'Claire has written an importa[...]
very core to and very wron[...]
that the church is much worse than the world it sits within, but surely it should be so much better – a place of acceptance and openness, of love and forgiveness. In this well-structured book, Claire takes us through the anatomy of the "mask", and how to start taking it off. It's not about sharing everything with everyone, but it is about being who you are and who God has made you to be – and proud of it!'

Dr Rob Waller
Consultant Psychiatrist, author and director
of the Mind and Soul Foundation

'This is an important book. If there is a safe environment for people to open up their lives, it ought to be the church. But the church is full of broken sinful people who are all on a journey of being redeemed, and often we are not sensitive to one another's needs. I found this book extremely enlightening.'

Wendy Virgo
Author

'When I was director of a counselling service for some ten years, it saddened me how often Christians presented for counselling when they could have received significant help in their own churches had they felt safe to lower their masks to those around them. Claire has addressed an important topic both in an informed way and with a considerable amount of brave disclosure about her own story.'

Jeannie Kendall
Co-minister at Carshalton Beeches Baptist Church
and formerly director of Manna Counselling

'Claire is an experienced, excellent writer with much to share. I was really interested in her experiences (as a minister's wife) and she made me think hard about our experiences and question how far I've been able to be me.'

Michele Guinness
Author and speaker

'For some reason we have created an "I am fine" culture in church today, yet every single one of us has times of feeling weak, fearful, confused, ashamed, miserable, anxious or angry. When we are honest and share those feelings we can connect with those around us; we start to share often the things that make us human, so share our common humanity. This is a crucial book that can help us to do just that.'

Patrick Regan OBE
Founder & CEO of XLP

'God has taken Claire on an amazing journey of discovering authentic Christian honesty. This book offers a brilliant insight into that journey. Step on board.'

Phil Moore
Pastor and author

'Finding the strength to be vulnerable about our weaknesses, our fears and our failures is tough, but Claire starts *Taking Off the Mask* with raw honesty as she leads us on a journey to authentic living. This book will challenge you, but it will lead you to a life free of other people's expectations on your life.'

Bekah Legg
Director of Mission at Maybridge Community Church
and editor of *Liberti* magazine

'Finally a book that confronts the shame factor attached to perfectionism – the epidemic that has gone undiagnosed for too long within the church. In Claire's honest account of her own experience in discovering authenticity, I am left with hope that the reader could contribute to a new movement by unveiling the people behind the masks – people who are liberated, powerful – accessing the original design of who they were always meant to be.'

Carrie Lloyd
Pastor and author

'Why do we make sacred cows out of marriage, parenting and finance – never letting people know it's all cracking until it's too late? If only we could create a culture where it is normal to talk about surface cracks, we might avoid the complete brokenness later on. I am so glad Claire has provided some practical and biblical steps to help people forwards.'

Cathy Madavan
Communications Consultant, speaker, a member of the
Spring Harvest planning team and author

'This is a fascinating and important book – one that is extremely timely for so many men and women in the church and beyond. I'm sure it will help all those who read it.'

Chine McDonald
Head of Christian Influence and Engagement
at World Vision UK

Claire Musters has written a courageous, vulnerable and wise book about the integral issue of authenticity in Christian community. Her candour invites us to join the journey of freedom in living with unveiled faces before God and others. Through careful research, engaging narrative, and soul-stirring reflection questions, Claire shows herself to be a trustworthy guide through tender terrain.'

Sharon Garlough Brown
Author and spiritual director

'This is such an important subject for the church and one close to my heart. As a society and as the church we desperately need to rediscover how to build authentic relationships. Change is possible. It starts with us. Claire Musters shows us how with vulnerability, wisdom and grace. She has a lovely writing style, easy to read, and I like the way she mixes her personal story with helpful information and ideas of how we might do things differently.'

Sarah Abell
Founder of NakedHedgehogs.com
and author

'Claire has written with the kind of honesty and compassion that touches hearts and changes lives. Her book is brimming with biblical truth and grace alongside her personal story; it will be such an encouragement to Christians seeking holy authenticity.'

Celia Bowring
Co-founder of CARE, writer and speaker

Taking Off the Mask

Daring to be the person
God created you to be

Claire Musters

Authentic

23 22 21 20 19 18 17   7 6 5 4 3 2 1

First published 2017 by Authentic Media Limited,
PO Box 6326, Bletchley, Milton Keynes, MK1 9GG.
authenticmedia.co.uk

British Library Cataloguing in Publication Data
A catalogue record for this book is available from the British Library.
ISBN: 978-1-78078-191-4
978-1-78078- 192-1 (e-book)

Cover design by Vivian Hansen
Printed and bound in the UK by CPI Group (UK) Ltd., Croydon, CR0 4YY

Contents

Foreword

I'm not a morning person, which is a benign way of saying that in the hours shortly after dawn I (a) communicate in grunts (b) absolutely never smile and (c) at times look somewhat dishevelled, like Lazarus looked before Jesus stopped by and enabled him to vacate that rather smelly tomb.

This early-in-the-day morose disposition means that I am not exactly an animated breakfast guest. I live much of the time in America, a land of mountains, prairies and the horrifying habit of going out for breakfast with friends, thereby making it a social event. This has, at times, been a challenge. Engaging socially while barely awake is difficult. And this particular breakfast was very difficult, because, unbeknown to me, those who had invited me to breakfast had anticipated that I'd perform.

The night before, I'd preached in a church, and the communication had flowed rather well. I was quick-witted, spontaneous and colourful in my presentation. People had laughed freely and easily, and I'd come away from the evening pleased, encouraged . . . and exhausted. A restless night spent tossing and turning in a hotel bed seemingly designed by the devil had not helped, and now, sitting in a café contemplating the possibility of eating pancakes and eggs with a group of men from the very same church, I was quiet, slightly sullen and battling the temptation to put my head on the table and snore.

It was then that the comment came. The horrifyingly jolly chap sitting next to me stabbed a sausage with his fork, and then delivered a stunningly witty question: 'So Jeff, are you related to a warm, funny guy who is engaging and sharp? We saw that guy on the platform last night. You look a bit like him, but you're not like him this morning. Are you two related?' He stabbed the sausage again, with a vigour that was slightly alarming.

I sat there, searching for a riposte. He probably didn't intend his words to be as acerbic as they sounded, but his message was clear:

'What's wrong with you?

'Come on, be the platform guy that entertained us last evening. Wake up. Tell us a story. Be that guy.'

I sighed inwardly, gathered strength and, at the next opportunity in the conversation, a miracle happened. Lazarus was raised. I told a witty story and everyone laughed. The performer was back at the table. But, as the breakfast ended, I went back to my hotel room with a heavy heart. Like a performing seal with a multi-coloured beach-ball on its nose, I'd delivered. But all that beach-ball balancing is hard work. They wanted breakfast with a clown on command, and so, rather than disappoint, I'd slapped on the make-up, and donned the ginger wig.

At one level of course, it was no big deal, but some of us go through our whole lives feeling the need to perform. Playing to the demands of others, covering our disappointments, veneering over the cracks of our doubts, we never show the real us, which is a shame, seeing as God crafted the real us. Some of us just do it to survive.

And of course, this is not just about us. God gets irked by consistent mask donning. In New Testament times, there were travelling bands of thespians who went into communities and performed plays, sometimes using masks to heighten the drama. They were called the *hypokrites*. It was this word that Jesus borrowed to expose the academy-award-level religious posturing of the Pharisees. Hypocrites.

Whatever our motive, living life with a mask is a very awkward, exhausting, unfulfilling way to live.

And that's why I welcome this book. With courageous, raw honesty, Claire Musters shares her own story of living life with various masks. I commend her for her vulnerability, and pray for her as she goes public: the sharing of self births both relief and rawness; we're glad to have peeked out from behind the façade, but we feel somewhat exposed as we do. But this finely crafted page-turner of a book does more than just confess: it gently nudges us to reflection and action, and calls us to a healthier way of living. The pathway Claire points to won't always be easy to navigate, but it leads us to a golden, jewel-studded palace – the beautiful place where we can be us.

So congratulations, Claire. Perhaps, at some time in the future, we can catch up over a meal and you'll surely be able to tell me how many people have been cheered, encouraged and blessed as a result of your undeniably beautiful book. I look forward to that. But please do me a favour: let's make it any meal but breakfast.

Jeff Lucas

To Steve – I know it was a hard decision,
but I so appreciate you allowing me to share our story.
I'm so grateful that I get to journey with you
as we continue to learn more about living mask-free.

To Mum – your resilient faith continues to inspire me.

Introduction

'I thought other Christians might do something like this – but not her.'

That sentence was said about me, after a very public mistake I made that rocked our small congregation to the core. My response to it, however, was to think, '*Really*? Had they really got me so wrong?'

My husband Steve and I were part of a team leading a church plant into the town in which we lived. We'd been married for almost a decade and, although we tried to keep it hidden, things in our marriage were rocky – and had been pretty much from the start. Occasionally I vocalized the need to share our difficulties with a third party, but my husband wasn't at that place yet. So I kept quiet, the very idea of people knowing how bad it had got was enough to persuade me that silence was the better option. But, with the hours Steve worked as a record producer, and my intensifying feelings of loneliness, our relationship was a pressure cooker getting ready to explode. And, yes, it did.

In an extremely messy episode the mask I had so obviously been wearing was literally ripped from me (totally against my will), and one of the hardest things I had to do was face my church community again.

Through that exceedingly painful time, I learned lessons that have remained with me. I also had the starting spark of a passion to see other Christians take their masks off long enough to be open and vulnerable with one another. I have been on a journey ever since, discovering more about what it means to live authentically and honestly.

This is a story of redemption, but also one that charts my own journey towards authentic living, which began when I discovered my own mask. Since then I've learned about the many other reasons we choose to conceal our real selves from those around us. I've also spent time exploring the ways in which I believe God encourages us to remove our masks and the tools he gives us to keep living mask-free.

How to use this book

I have broken the book into three distinct parts. In the first I share the moment when I realized I had been wearing a mask, and the impact that knowledge began to have on me.

The second part focuses on the reasons why we wear masks. Each one of us will wear a mask that we have crafted for ourselves, probably over a number of years, so it will be unique. However, the reasons for creating those masks in the first place are often based in issues of identity and the difficult circumstances that we've faced. Since looking into the subject more closely, I've discovered that our mask-wearing often starts very early on in life, and can be a learned behaviour, too. So I start by looking at our upbringing, personalities and the culture we live in, before turning to subjects such as disappointment, fear and rejection.

It is those core reasons for mask-wearing that I feel we need to recognize for ourselves and start to deal with, before we can take the first steps to removing our own mask. Part Three then moves on to cover general encouragements to help us begin this whole process, and progresses to learning how to keep the mask off. In both these parts I include personal reflections at the end of each chapter, which I hope will help you to put the ideas into the context of your own life.

Just a quick point of clarification: when I talk about masks, I am referring to those covers we use to protect our vulnerable selves, or particular personas we decide to project to others while keeping the rest of ourselves hidden. It is that sense of hiding ourselves away that I long for us to break free from. So, in this book, I am focusing on when our masks have become either a distortion of who we really are or are completely covering over our true selves.

My heart for this book is that each of you will go on your own journey into greater authenticity as you read it. You may not be aware that you wear a mask, or the reasons why, because mask-wearing can often happen subconsciously. I am praying that the Holy Spirit will reveal to you any areas in which you are concealing your real self as you work through the book.

On the other hand, you may already know exactly why you wear a mask, so please feel free to dip straight into the relevant chapter if you are eager to do so. However, journeying through the book as a whole will help you to understand more about not only yourself, but those around you too. I was surprised to find, as I delved deeper into the subjects I've covered (particularly in Part Two), God revealing certain things to me about myself for the very first time. I pray he will provide you with such insights too.

Ultimately, I hope and pray this book will give you the courage to walk into deeper freedom, and encourage those around you to do so too.

You are not alone

Through my own journey, I have come to understand that we *all* struggle at times. It was certainly a relief to finally 'get' that, as for so long I had looked at others and compared the reality of my own life with what I thought theirs was like. I felt con-demned because I seemed to always come up short. But I also believe it is partly *because of* our struggles that God encourages us to meet together regularly.

When we become Christians we are born into God's family and it *should* be a safe and caring environment. I know that, unfortunately, that isn't always the case. However, many of us wear our masks like protective shells, more concerned about keeping ourselves free of hurt than reaching out to connect with others. I do believe that God wants to help us gently prise those masks away, bit by bit, so that we can face him as we truly are – and realize that we are totally loved and fully accepted. When we learn to bask in his love, mercy and grace we can't help but be transformed – and this will impact our relationships with others too.

PART ONE

DISCOVERING THE 'REAL ME' BENEATH THE MASK

I want to start this book by being truly honest about my own personal story. It's where my journey into authenticity began and is the reason for this book. Within these pages I'll be encouraging you to dig deep and find out why you wear a mask, as well as suggesting steps you can take to help you remove it and reveal the real you – so the least I can do is share with you the journey that has led me to this point. You'll learn about the many mistakes I've made and the struggles I can still have. I'm hoping this will give you hope and courage for your own situation, because we each need to give ourselves permission to delve beneath our masks, to discover, acknowledge and give ourselves time to work through any disappointments, hurts, grief, etc. we may have experienced. It is only then that we can truly walk in freedom. So here is my story . . .

Donning My Mask

I know the name of the main mask that I wore for over a decade: 'victim'. I allowed it to become my identity as it resonated so deeply within me.

Before I put on that particular mask, on the surface my life seemed to be all neatly packaged up. I worked hard at school and university, earned a first-class honours degree and landed a job I was really interested in. While at university I married my childhood sweetheart and, to top everything off, we were both Christians. What a wonderfully romantic, 'perfect' set-up . . . And yet that was part of the problem. Everyone else thought our lives were so sorted that we felt we had to do everything we could to live up to that façade (the ever popular 'I'm fine'/'I'm in control' mask). Steve in particular felt uncomfortable with people knowing the truth about how difficult we were finding things.

I, on the other hand, moaned about how hard our marriage was. *A lot.* Mainly to my husband and to God, but also to those closest to me that I found gave me sympathy. (Anyone who challenged me stopped being someone I would confide in.) I spent years hiding my identity behind that smokescreen of being a victim. It affected everything I did – everything I believed.

Looking back now, I'm shocked at how much it affected me, but at the time I thought I was completely justified. I was basically saying to myself, 'My life is in limbo because my husband isn't here.'

I had known that getting married at a young age and to a man who had just entered the music business would be difficult, but I never really stopped to contemplate how hard it may be. As I said to my mum when she tried to talk through the implications with me: 'It's too late. I fell in love with him years before he got his job.' And so we embarked on marriage, with me refusing to do marriage preparation classes because I would have ended up doing them on my own as Steve was always working. Of course, this meant I was still full of my childhood's romantic notions about what marriage should be like, as I hadn't let anyone systematically challenge my warped views and set them right.

And then the reality hit.

Coping with my final year at university and with a husband who literally worked twenty-plus hours a day, six or seven days a week, I became incredibly lonely, frustrated and, yes, bitter. I cried out to God, asking him why he had brought us together, allowed us to be married, just for me to become a studio widow.

God's answer was one I didn't want to hear. He told me, gently, that he would be my husband, and that he wanted to woo me and teach me what it would be like to rely on him for everything.

My response? I shouted at him that I didn't want him for my husband. He wouldn't be there to hold when I needed a hug, and I couldn't sit face to face and chat with him. God just didn't seem physical enough at the time. I *needed* Steve there, for me. So I rebelled, and I allowed every situation and circumstance I faced to be seen through the victim mask that I began to wear. It coloured my view of everything.

I can remember spending some time in intense ministry during which the burden of those years was lifted off me, and I was told that the years the locusts had eaten would be restored.[1] And I can see now that, even in my response to that moment, I was still viewing everything through the same mentality. I was still believing that what had happened had happened *to* me; that I was helpless in it all.

But of course, so much of what happened was down to my choices. *I chose* to move away from God, and from church for a time. *I chose* to throw myself into work when I started working in a publishing company. *I chose* to socialize with colleagues every evening, getting home just before bedtime each night and then getting up to start the cycle again.

By keeping myself busy, I didn't have to deal with the gaping hole I felt inside. But I was masking my true identity by identifying with those who made me feel more comfortable. I was drawn to those who empathized with me and fed my victim mentality with phrases such as, 'It is outrageous that you, such a young wife, have basically been abandoned.'

> I was masking my true identity by identifying with those who made me feel more comfortable.

I was being fed what I wanted to hear, so naturally I lapped it all up. It was very easy to accept and feed on it – and yet all it did was make things worse.

I continued on a self-destructive cycle for a few years, until eventually I realized that I was miserable and needed to get right with God in order to regain my inner peace. I began to prioritize my walk with him again and became much more involved in the church we were attending at the time. I ended up on the worship team and ran a life group alongside another woman whose husband worked ridiculously long hours. I believe that was all preparation for the early years of the church we helped to start. Unfortunately, I hadn't dealt with the root of the problem and that victim mask still had a hold on me. I may have taken it off for a while, but it wasn't long before it was luring me to pick it back up . . .

My Unmasking

Unfortunately, my victim identity grew from its root and crept into our lives again at different times. A few years after I had become much more involved in church, we moved a short distance to be where a new church was going to be started. We were also part of the initial leadership team.[1] But not long before we were going to officially launch the church, my victim mentality gripped me again. Instead of telling it where to go, I embraced it, like an old glove that fitted me so well.

Sadly, this put me in danger of allowing my emotional needs to be fed by other sources. Over time, a friendship with another man in my church, which had started innocently enough, intensified to a different level. We decided to leave everything behind and start a new life together. With our actions we devastated the lives of his wife, my husband and all the other members of our close-knit church community.

Although I did not recognize it as such at the time, God's grace was at work and, two weeks later, the man chose to go back to his wife. This meant I was left alone and broken, standing with the proverbial egg on my face, with a husband whose heart was shattered and a group of people who had trusted me now working through shock, pain and how to forgive. I felt as if my mask had been yanked right off me and I was left exposed and vulnerable. The worst part was that I knew I deserved it all.

Tellingly, it was Steve whom I rang once the other guy left. He had been my best friend since I was a teenager, so I called him without even thinking. He left work immediately to come to me. How hard it must have been for him to then take me back home, and watch me huddled in the foetal position, sobbing endlessly. The next day he moved me and a lot of my belongings to my parents' home, where I was to stay until I had healed enough to discover what was next for my life.

I had lost everything by wrongfully pinning my hopes on another human being, rather than God. And I was like a wounded animal at times – licking my wounds, lashing out, wanting to be left alone. I can't imagine what it must have been like for Steve going home, getting up for work each day and not knowing whether our marriage was salvageable.

Of course, we had deep issues that needed dealing with, within our marriage. But I had to get to a place, first, of believing there was a future there at all, and that I could look past all the years of hurt and misunderstanding and repent, as well as forgive, and move on. My husband needed to do the same, although I know that God had been working on his heart the whole time I was away and he was more than willing to start the process of restoration.

When Steve visited me I felt a little suffocated at times, as I knew he was trying his best to win me back. But most of the time he was gracious, gentle and loving, and knew when to give me space. How he responded to me during that difficult time of limbo taught me what real love is. He

> That humbling experience has left an imprint of grace on my heart forever.

revealed Jesus' love for me in a very tangible way. That humbling experience has left an imprint of grace on my heart forever.

Yes, we had counselling. And yes, we *both* had to face up to our failings, to understand the responsibility we had for one another and the changes that needed to occur. But my husband's gentle patience during that time melted my hardened, broken heart. He was a solid anchor who remained firm, even during those times when the pain of what had happened pierced his heart afresh. After I had moved back home, there would still be moments when I would be wracked with emotional pain all over again and he would just hold me, caring for me through the tears.

Confronting who I was

I know that being honest and open can be painful. It certainly wasn't my choice to begin with. It was thrust upon me when I was forced to face the consequences of my actions. I know that up until that point people had thought I was mature, viewed me as a leader and believed I was trustworthy, so they were hurt by my actions and we all needed to work through how I had made us feel. While some may say I had worn leadership like a mask, I do believe God had called me to be doing what I was doing. Sadly, I had just kept the hurting, scared inner person locked inside rather than sharing her and getting the right sort of help. Once everything was revealed for what it was, I desperately needed my church's understanding, love, gentleness and forgiveness.

One friend said he'd had an inkling of what was going to happen before it did, and wished he had confronted me months before. At the time I was alarmed that such a thought had crossed his mind, as I have no idea how I would have reacted. Since then, I've wondered what it was that stopped him – and why we can all seem to struggle with asking each other the questions that get right to the heart of what is going on in our lives.

Losing my mask was a scary, difficult experience during which, at times, I felt totally lost – and I had to face the possibility that the life I'd had previously may have gone forever. (At the time, I wasn't sure my marriage could be put back together, or if my friends – and the church – would welcome me back.) But believe me, I grew up a lot in that period. I was forced to face my fears, as well as acknowledge my weaknesses and sinful tendencies. I had nowhere else to go, so there was simply no point trying to run from it all any more. I *had* to confront who I was, and where I was currently at. Although it was painful, I knew that God was at work, doing 'surgery' in my inner being, cutting out the parts that had been allowed to go toxic for so long.

Learning in the wilderness

Looking back on that period, I can see how it was one of my biggest wilderness experiences. I had been taken out of my life's context, and was battling for life as I knew it. Turning to Jesus' time in the desert I found I was able to learn some things that really spoke into my own life.

Firstly, Jesus was led by the Spirit into the wilderness to be tempted. God was in control of what was happening. Jesus was being stripped in the process of being made ready for his ministry. He was taken out of his circumstances, was even forgoing any kind of sustenance, but he was there with the Holy Spirit, who would guide him through the whole experience. That was so helpful to

me, as I felt I had been taken out (through my own sin) just at a piv-
otal time in our church's history. I felt I had failed and was no longer
of any use. But here I was learning how Jesus was being prepared
for his ministry through a time of being away from everything.

The devil tried to undermine Jesus' identity and calling
through his carefully chosen temptations. He waited until the
end of Jesus' forty days, when Jesus would have been at his most
hungry and therefore most vulnerable. He also tried to get him
to focus on his own strength – luring him into turning stones
into bread. Jesus knew where to find his sustenance (in the word
of God) and refused to give in to any of the devil's temptations.

Interestingly, in Matthew 4:4 Jesus quotes Deuteronomy 8.
Turning to that I saw afresh how God has made it his business
to reveal humans' hearts and motivations to them – and has
disciplined them out of love and care:

> Remember how the LORD your God led you all the way in the wil-
> derness these forty years, to humble and test you in order to know
> what was in your heart, whether or not you would keep his com-
> mands. He humbled you, causing you to hunger and then feeding
> you with manna, which neither you nor your ancestors had known,
> to teach you that man does not live on bread alone but on every
> word that comes from the mouth of the LORD. Your clothes did not
> wear out and your feet did not swell during these forty years. Know
> then in your heart that as a man disciplines his son, so the LORD your
> God disciplines you (Deut. 8:2–5).

Throughout the Israelites' forty years wandering in the desert,
he provided for their physical needs. I knew that he was going
to hold me and restore me through my own desert experience,
even though it was painful and included discipline.

As part of the process of rebuilding my life, I used to walk along the beach near my parents' house and work through my difficulties with God. Spending time gazing out at the majestic enormity of the sea put things into perspective for me. Each day the tide ebbed and flowed and the huge waves crashed onto the rocks. And each day I was reminded how small and insignificant my life is.

And yet.

God also reminded me that he loves me and is interested in the minutest details of my life. He wants to converse with me, guide me and direct me. He wants to be the first person I turn to in the morning and the last person I speak with before sleeping at night.

I began to realize that I had had unrealistic expectations when I got married. I had somehow viewed my husband as my sole spiritual leader and thereby washed my own hands of responsibility. I had expected him to do certain things that he obviously wasn't able to while he was working so hard in the studio. But, in a contradictory manner, I'm quite capable so I forged ahead, making spiritual and other decisions that affected our home without fully talking issues over with Steve.

As God had told me all those years ago, he wanted to teach me to lean on him utterly and completely. So, in that time away from home, I simply learned to submit to his gentle guiding and let him teach me what to do.

Finding freedom

I had to start from scratch, rebuilding my life completely. I needed to reconstruct my relationship with God, my relationship with Steve – the one man who has truly reflected Jesus' love for me in the way he has dealt with my mistakes – and my friendships with those in the church.

It was a long, difficult process, but I have to say it was also incredibly freeing.

I was so scared of returning home – of going back to our church. I had no idea how people would react to me. (I was rather perturbed that God was telling me I had to go back – it would have been far easier to hide from it all. I also had to battle through forgiving the man I had left Steve for, when he was getting off scot-free – which is how I originally viewed it. He and his wife found a new church and eventually moved away.)

Coming to the point of realizing we should stay in our church community was not a lightning-bolt-from-the-sky moment. Steve had taken me away to Italy for my thirtieth birthday and one of the things on our agenda was praying through our future now we were back together. Did it mean a move from the town we lived in? Should we change churches so that we could start afresh?

We spent a rather frustrating week of seeking hard after God but hearing nothing, until one day he gently spoke to me and said, 'Have I told you to move?'

We had been very sure of God's original calling to move to help start the church we were now at, and God was simply re-confirming that. It was a hard thing to swallow, but also wonderful to know that he hadn't discounted us from our calling because of the huge mistakes we'd made.

When I finally returned to church, I was petrified of walking through the door, but the grace, forgiveness and love I was shown overwhelmed me. And being amongst people that now knew the worst about me, and yet still accepted and loved me, was just what I needed to continue the healing process.

Our church community has since grown and developed and, after a period of time working part-time in the music industry and part-time helping out our pastor, Steve now leads it. Even though many years have passed, I sometimes still look around and think how strange it is that there are people there that don't know everything about my past! That's fine by me though – I just need to make sure that I don't pick my mask back up and slip it on, as it has a tendency to look so inviting.

Learning from Jesus

I have said that the way that Steve responded to me, stubbornly refusing to give up loving me, revealed Jesus' acceptance of me in a whole new way. It helped me to truly understand that, however far I fell, I would never be too far out of reach of the steadying hand of Jesus. I saw the verse in Psalm 139 about the depths ('if I make my bed in the depths, you are there' v.8) in a new light. Even when I chose to walk my own way, and ended up in those depths through my own bad decisions, he pursued me and pulled me back out.

Not only was I beginning to comprehend that I am fully accepted by him, but I began to see that the authenticity I longed for could be found reflected in Jesus' life. I have already shared how I felt such a connection with his time in the wilderness. But there is so much more Jesus has to teach me about authenticity.

Even today, each time I look more closely at the gospels, I see the honesty that I crave in the way Jesus interacted with others. He drew a close-knit group of people around him and wasn't afraid to be vulnerable with them. He taught his disciples to be radical in the way that they lived too. They were

> I see the honesty that I crave in the way Jesus interacted with others.

full of doubts and mistakes and weren't afraid to voice them. Did that mean he discounted them? No. He fully accepted them, gently (and sometimes not so gently!) corrected them and taught them how to be the leaders of the church they would serve after his resurrection.

Resonating with Peter

Since discovering my mask, I have found the example of Peter particularly encouraging. That is probably because there are echoes of my own story in the way that Jesus unceremoniously unmasked his hidden fears and agendas. He did it because he loved Peter – and because it needed doing (just as it did in my life). Look, for example, at what happens in Mark 14. Jesus has just told his disciples that he will be betrayed by one of them. Peter doesn't like the way the conversation has gone, especially when Jesus tells them that they will all 'fall away'. He puts on a mask of bravado and pride and unrealistically and categorically says that he will follow Jesus to the death rather than deny him. Jesus' take on the situation? He clearly states what will happen – that before the cock crows for a second time Peter will deny him three times.

Interestingly, straight after this, they go to Gethsemane where Jesus wrestles with what he is about to endure. But, while Peter has been determined to show himself in a good light, Jesus is happy to be totally vulnerable with his disciples about what a heavy burden he is carrying, 'My soul is overwhelmed with sorrow to the point of death' (v.34). He asks them simply to stay nearby and keep watch.

When he is alone, we see how Jesus is willing to be totally honest with his Father too. He asks if there is any way God can rescue humanity without him having to be crucified, but then he submits to God's will. This is a great model for how we should be with our heavenly Father too – honest, yet humbly submitting to his sovereignty.

When Jesus returns to his disciples, he finds them sleeping, and specifically gives Peter a further warning: 'Watch and pray so that you will not fall into temptation' (v.38). And yet, when Jesus is taken, Peter immediately allows fear to overtake him and he follows 'at a distance' (v.54). When he is questioned by a servant girl who recognizes him, he then denies who he truly is. He had given over his life to following Jesus, spending his days with him and calling himself his disciple. And yet he so quickly denies all that by stating that he never knew Jesus. When the cock crows for the second time, the mask suddenly drops and Peter realizes what he has done (v.72).

Peter must have left that scene still full of anguish and shame – and then he went on to watch his beloved Jesus die such a cruel death. How excruciatingly painful. And what guilt he must have carried alongside his grief in the days that followed. What I love about Jesus, though, is the way he restores people. Once resurrected, he appears to the disciples. The first time he does, he opens doubting Thomas's eyes by showing him the marks in his hands and side (see John 20:24–29).

John's gospel also includes a revealing episode in which Jesus appears to the disciples again, this time while they are fishing. He makes a point of drawing alongside Peter, and through a tough but beautiful cleansing conversation shows Peter that he forgives and restores him (John 21:15–17). Jesus asks him three times whether he loves him. Three times for the three denials.

The first two times, the Greek word he uses for love is *agape*, which means self-sacrificial love. The first time it is in the context of the group; the second, he is focusing on just Peter. The third time the word Jesus uses is *phileis*, from the word *philos*, which means beloved or friend. Here Jesus is talking about brotherly affection. I believe, through this process, he is asking Peter to both confront his past mistakes and look honestly at what his true feelings and motivations are. Jesus uses this to redeem Peter and charges him with the task of looking after the church: 'feed my sheep' (v.17).

Living honestly

Through what I have faced in my own life, and learned by look-ing at Jesus', I have come to believe passionately that God wants us to live transparent, honest lives. This involves recognizing and facing our shortcomings, as Jesus encouraged Peter to do, as well as being real with those around us about our lows as well as our highs. I am so glad that God provides acres of grace and mercy for when we do mess up – and that he champions our efforts to be authentic.

> God champions our efforts to be authentic.

The sad thing is, too often we can act out a part that we be-lieve is expected of us, rather than truly living in the freedom that God's love brings. He delights in us and wants us to enjoy the experience of being ourselves, and yet so often we can be trapped in an unnecessary cycle of pretence. God never de-mands it of us, and sometimes it takes real effort to keep up the façade. There are times when we long just to be able to be real with someone – anyone. And yet the mask stays on and we con-tinue pretending everything is okay. We are going to explore why that happens in the next part of this book.

PART TWO

WHY *DO* WE WEAR MASKS IN CHURCH?

We wear the mask that grins and lies,
It hides our cheeks and shades our eyes, –
This debt we pay to human guile;
With torn and bleeding hearts we smile,
And mouth with myriad subtleties.

Why should the world be over-wise,
In counting all our tears and sighs?
Nay, let them only see us, while
We wear the mask.

We smile, but, O great Christ, our cries
To thee from tortured souls arise.
We sing, but oh the clay is vile
Beneath our feet, and long the mile;
But let the world dream otherwise,
We wear the mask!

> *'We Wear the Mask'*
> *Paul Laurence Dunbar (1872–1906)*

WHY DO WE WEAR MASKS
IN CHURCH?

Discovering Reasons for Our Masks

I talked about the love and grace that I received when I went back to our church community for the first time after Steve and I got back together. That is totally true – and yet there was more to the story, because I was always conscious of the fact that I was walking around 'naked', exposed. Everybody knew what depths I had sunk to; what I was really capable of.

As the weeks went by I would go to meetings in small-group settings and feel God prompt me to be honest and open with those around me. But it felt raw, harsh and lonely. Over time, I began to realize why: no one else had lowered their mask. I was making myself extremely vulnerable but it seemed I was journeying on my own. I really wrestled through that experience, at times being almost toddler-like in my exclamations of 'It's not fair to make just me do it!' to God. And yet, bit by bit, I saw others respond to my openness. Some said to me: 'I thought it was just me,' while others admitted, 'I was worried about what people would think.' Through this process I began to gain more understanding of

> I was making myself extremely vulnerable but it seemed I was journeying on my own.

why, when our churches are supposed to be safe places, so many of us continue to don our masks inside them.

Since discovering my mask-wearing wasn't unique to me, I have been much more aware of the possible reasons why we seem to feel safer keeping our masks on in church. I have spent the last decade or so really exploring these, looking at what the Bible tells us and also learning from speakers and teachers who have particular insights into areas such as disappointment and suffering.

Asking others

As part of my research for this book I wanted to hear from other Christians who don't go to the same church as me, to find out what their experiences have been like. I put together a survey, asking people to honestly assess whether they feel they can be themselves in their own church community and, if not, to indicate the reasons they feel they can't.[1] These ranged from: 'Most Christians cannot be trusted with total confidentiality. They think it is okay to talk to someone else about other people's problems (without their permission) as long as they pray about them,' right through to the very sad: 'I've been hurt too much in the past – I've given up on church.' Some of the other answers are included in the chapters in this part of the book.

What I found most sobering from my survey findings was that less than a third of those who responded said they felt they could be themselves in church. A third said they could only be real with close friends and the rest felt they could only reveal a little of themselves – or nothing at all. Although this is, of course, only a small sample of people, it is so sad to think of how many people there *could* be in our churches today that feel uncomfortable, unsafe and unable to truly relax and be themselves.

Understanding ourselves

As I said in the Introduction, it was interesting to discover that most of the reasons people feel unable to reveal their true selves are based in issues of identity. How we are perceived by others – and how we are treated by them too – has a huge influence on how authentic we feel we can be in any given setting. This influence can be exerted early on, with the messages our caregivers share with us, but remains a big factor throughout our lives. But what is it about fear, rejection, disappointment, shame and so on that can grip us and cause us to hold our masks tightly to our faces? We can be desperate to hide behind them,

> The masks are actually suffocating the real people – the real you and me – that are trapped behind them.

even though they are limiting our experience of life. In fact, the masks are actually suffocating the real people – the real you and me – that are trapped behind them.

I will be looking at these factors, and many more, in this part of the book. I reveal my own struggles with them as well as the stories friends have been honest and brave enough to tell me, and allow me to include. I also unpack some of the most helpful Bible verses I have found for combatting these reasons, as well as share teaching that has inspired and encouraged me in my own walk towards mask-free living.

Really understanding our own particular reasons for choosing to put a mask on is the first step to being able to make a decision to take it off. Many of the reasons for mask-wearing are quite complicated, and far-reaching. With God's help, we need to tackle what lies beneath them for us as individuals. I hope and pray that the things I share in this part of the book will help you to begin to do that. As I say many times, it may be helpful for you to ask someone else to come alongside you as you process your own particular reasons for mask-wearing – whether a friend, church leader or counsellor. God is ever gentle and merciful: as you are about to embark on this part of the book, why not ask him to open your eyes to see what he wants to reveal to you?

The Role of Upbringing

I often mask who I truly am in order to blend in. I have come to realize that this may have been a learned behaviour that I picked up, in part, during my childhood, as we moved a lot due to my father's job. Every few years I had to say goodbye to friends and cultivate new relationships in the place that we had moved to.

When I look back now, I have fond memories of that period. I am grateful for the interesting places I was able to travel to and discover, and for the people I met. But there is one memory that vividly comes to mind, because it caused me to want to crawl inside myself and hide from those I was surrounded by. It happened as I walked into a new classroom in England, having just moved back from America. I was the second child to start the term late – a boy from Australia had started a few days before me.

The first phrase I heard when I entered my new class was, 'Oh no. Not another one.'

The heckler was obviously oblivious to the subtle intricacies of different accents, but I remember the flush of embarrassment and the overwhelming desire just to be given a place to sit. I was desperate to simply 'lose' myself amongst the other children, rather than be standing in front of them like a bizarre exhibit. Within a few days I had replaced my heavy American accent with one that wouldn't mark me out every time I spoke.

I can sometimes *still* sense that feeling of trepidation as I walk into a room full of people I do not know. Even at a recent conference, where I knew the delegates all shared the same interests as me (they were all writers and Christians), the moment I set foot inside the hall, I wanted to turn around and flee. It was only when I located some people I had already connected with on the internet that I felt able to relax a little. I know some of that is down to my personality (the subject of the next chapter), but I can sometimes allow the fear of a repeat of that mortifying moment to overtake me.

Putting these two particular episodes side by side is a simple example of how much our childhood experiences can influence our behaviour as adults. While thinking about our childhood and how that can impact our behaviour today is fairly new to me, psychologists and psychiatrists have studied such links for years.

One child psychiatrist, John Bowlby, asserted that we all have an innate primary fear of rejection, because we're all wired for relationships as part of our survival mechanism. One of the main reasons many of us wear masks, myself included, is to protect ourselves from rejection by others (see Chapter 9). Having to make friends over and over again as a young child, often put me in the firing line of rejection. While I did make good friends in each new place we settled, there were those who didn't accept me. As a shy, fairly gawky child, I was never part of the 'cool' groups.

Psychologists believe, however, that the influences on our behaviour go back even further than our early friendships, to our very first relationships or 'attachments'.

Learning how to relate to others

Bowlby penned the 'Attachment Theory', which states that each of us forms close, emotional attachments to one or two individuals who care for us from birth. These attachments will be either secure or insecure, based on the interactions we have with those caregivers during childhood. A secure attachment will help to meet our deep inner need for security, self-worth and significance.

> A secure attachment will help to meet our deep inner need for security, self-worth and significance.

This was something that I really began to unpack when I was co-writing another book. I learned that the vital importance of receiving this sense of security within childhood is why God put us in families:

> Our emotional tanks are empty when we are born but get filled up in a loving, fully functioning family. Research in places like Romania shows us how important this actually is. In Romanian orphanages it has been found that when children feel abandoned rather than loved and cared for they don't develop their security and sense of worth and, as a result, don't survive very well.[1]

Our early attachments give us a framework on which to base our own sense of self, as well as the model for forging relationships throughout our whole lives.

The way those early caregivers respond to us shapes our expectations for how others will treat us in the future – and teaches us how to relate to others ourselves.[2] We all long for relationship, and our early experiences teach us what relationships look like. This means that we often unknowingly seek out, or conduct, relationships similar to those we've experienced as children, because that is what has been modelled to us and so has become our 'norm'. Many of us replay a similar 'script' in our inter-actions with the different people that we

> We all long for relationship, and our early experiences teach us what relationships look like.

meet throughout our lives. This replaying may well involve mask-wearing, if we feel we need to project a particular persona to relate to the other person involved.

Sue Gerhardt, who wrote the bestselling *Why Love Matters*, has provided a compelling assertion that the love and affection that we receive in infancy is vital for our emotional develop-ment. She believes that the way an infant is nurtured literally sets pathways for behaviour in the brain.

Sue explains that while the first year of life is about making connections in the brain, the following couple of years are about untangling and deciphering those connections on a 'use it or lose it' basis. So children who have lived with angry people, for example, will keep the pathways that allow them to be alert to aggressive behaviour. Those who have had attentive caregivers will keep the pathways that help them be attentive themselves.[3]

In some families there is a strong message that emotions are somehow wrong – the 'stiff upper lip' mentality, in which pain, anger, sadness, etc. are seen as bad. Any conversations about these emotions, and any ways of releasing them, are stifled. Many of us are taught that being emotional is a sign of weak-ness, and so we learn to push emotions down rather than being able to express them in a safe place. This becomes our default, and so we continue to stuff our emotions down throughout adulthood too, and have to work hard to overcome that.

It seems to follow quite naturally that people who have grown up in homes that taught them to hide their emotions will be well versed in wearing masks. But *any* early attachments that are insecure will deeply affect our overall sense of identity – including our sense of security, acceptance and worth. Without the loving, nurturing support of caring parents/adult figures in those formative years, we can retreat into ourselves and wear masks as an outer layer of protection, thus hiding the soft inner, hurting child.

It is fascinating to understand that those vital first few years really do teach us how to respond to others, based on the people we have been most attached to during that time. This could provide an understanding of why some of us don't feel safe in social situations. Past experiences within childhood in which caregivers did not treat us fairly or well can cause us to project a fear of that happening again into our adult interactions.

So, while each one of us begins to make our own choices more and more as we grow up, we can see that our lives are also heavily shaped by the choices other people have made – in the way they have related to us, and how they have taught us to relate to others in return. As a parent, I found this a sobering thought as it highlights my responsibility.

What is interesting is that, while we all instinctively look to those closest to us to meet our needs, some psychologists recognize that parents will *not* be able to satisfy our deep needs fully.[4] In fact, they assert that a sense of frustration about that is a good and natural part of the process of human development. If our caregiver was perfect at recognizing and meeting our every need it would eventually perpetuate a feeling of helplessness in us as individuals. This frustration also encourages us to seek out the only one who can *truly* satisfy. When we recognize this frustration for ourselves, we can choose to turn towards God, and also learn to offer up to him those parts of us that may have been hurt, overlooked or mistreated in our formative years. As our heavenly Father, he longs to reach that inner child in each one of us with his healing love; that part of us that recognizes our deep need of him.

The effect of an insecure attachment

My parents separated then divorced when I was very young (still a baby/toddler), and so my earliest memories are in fact of growing up with my mum and loving stepdad. He always showed that he wanted my sister and I through his actions, and I have grown up calling him 'dad'. Due to the stable home life that my parents worked hard to create right from the start of their new life together, I feel that I had a very secure childhood and felt accepted and encouraged at all times.[5]

I wanted to hear from someone who didn't have the same type of happy childhood, to help me understand further the effect of those very early insecure attachments. I connected with Joy through a Christian writers' group we both belong to. She is an amazing woman of grace and writes beautifully sensitive poetry,[6] but her childhood was extremely difficult and has continued to impact her in her adult years. I am so grateful that she has been willing to share her own personal experiences:

> Home didn't feel safe when I was growing up, largely due to experiencing emotional and sexual abuse in my formative years, and partly due to my parents' constant verbal sparring, trapped as they were in a loveless marriage of convenience. My mother sought to

escape as soon as she could; her leaving didn't shock or surprise me too much, because I was already aware that I was an unwanted, unwelcome encumbrance in her life.

The scars these experiences left behind caused me to deny the real person deep inside, to be introverted and shy, to hide away and pretend to be something other than who I really am, because I felt so unworthy of the right kind of love and attention. I also found myself seeking love and security in all the wrong places before I gave my life to Christ.

A painful past tends to remain rooted in us as adults, unless we allow God's grace to infiltrate, slowly heal and begin to erase the deep-seated feelings it leaves us with. Those include feelings of not being loved or good enough, of being unworthy and unwanted by our caregivers or parents, and therefore intrinsically (so we believe) by those we dare to let come close to us. It takes time, perseverance and faith to overcome a challenging childhood, and I'm still a work in progress to some extent. But lasting change and restoration are always possible with God's help.

The role of the inner voice

I found it so helpful to read Joy's honest reflections on the effect her childhood has had on her. I was interested to note that she seemed to have taken on board critical messages about herself; we are going to explore how that happens a little further.

During the process of working alongside Christian counsellor Chris Ledger,[7] I have discovered how, as children, we internalize the messages that we receive from our caregivers. Unfortunately, it is the negative messages that often 'speak' the loudest.

This, in turn, has a lasting effect on what we think about ourselves – as well as on how we treat ourselves. That voice inside our head that often judges us more harshly than those around us do is what counsel-

> It is the negative messages that often 'speak' the loudest.

lors and psychologists call our 'inner critical voice'.[8] It wants us to do well in the world around us and be liked by everyone, so it responds to what it has learned over time. In an effort to protect us (particularly our more vulnerable areas), it can go overboard and even begin to attack our sense of self and wellbeing as it simply does not know when to stop.

The messages our inner critical voice feeds our minds can become out of control, as it draws attention to every little mistake and fault it finds. This is different to the Holy Spirit conviction that we can sometimes experience. When we are convicted, it is to bring us to a place of repentance, which then facilitates freedom, whereas a negative inner critical voice heaps condemnation upon us.

The strong, unhelpful opinions our inner critical voice can have are often fed by what our parents/caregivers said to us (or modelled for us through their behaviour towards us). Our upbringing can affect how susceptible we are, for example, to comparing ourselves with others. If we were forever compared to our siblings/friends/neighbours' children then we may well have heard the actual words, 'Why can't you be more like them?' Our inner critical voice may have picked up on all this negative input and still be constantly drip-feeding us exactly the same message. As a result, we can wear a mask in an attempt to be more like the type of person our caregivers – and inner critical voice – seem to want us to be (whether that is actually the truth or not).

Society plays a part too

The wider society we grow up in will often reinforce the negative messages we hear too, as so much of it is based on performance, outward appearance and behaviour. For example, as children we are all evaluated, academically as well as in other areas such as sport, by how well we perform. If we have struggled in certain areas, the message from both school and home may be that we need to try to do better. Conversely, if we've excelled, we may have picked up on an unspoken pressure to maintain that level of performance. Again, our inner voice can keep that message at the forefront of our minds so that we never relax, always feel like a failure or always feel the need to put on a performance (and this can often happen subconsciously).

I know that, for myself, doing well at school drove me to work even harder. My closest school friends were also high achievers, and so there was always a sense of competition between us. That may have fuelled my tendency towards perfectionism, and I know I can put myself under a lot of pressure because of it. I also believe that the fact that I was sometimes bullied as a child, was always picked last for sports teams (not being naturally sporty) and had a PE teacher who liked to point out my faults helped to fuel my sense of worthlessness.

There is nothing worse than standing in front of your whole class, watching as team captains pick person after person, and overlook you again and again. As the sides grow larger the line empties, until you are the only one completely rejected, with all eyes looking back at you. Then the team you are allocated to sighs and you have to do the walk of shame over to them. Horrific. I still have shivers as I think about that experience, which was repeated over and over. Internalizing this message, of being useless and wanted by no one, grew into more of a problem in my teenage years when my inner voice constantly told me how unlovable I was. This occurred even though my parents continued to shower their love on me, as it was the messages from my peers that affected me most at that point.

Building walls

As we have seen, the way we respond to others, the 'role' that we can undertake in certain situations, and the masks that we put on in order to do so, will probably have been taught to us in childhood by those around us. Our attitudes will have been shaped in those years and many of us continue to wear the masks that were created during that time. While they may have served to protect us for a short while, in adulthood they can create walls between us and others (including God). The result is we are cut off from reaching a deeper level of knowing others and being known ourselves. However, the same need for love and acceptance is just as strong for us as adults as it was when we were children. We can feel either positively enriched by the relationships we have . . . or let down by them. I have come to believe that it is helpful to learn to navigate both our good and bad experiences, and to realize when the more difficult ones cause us to retreat under our masks for protection.

We can find it difficult to recognize the relational masks that we use, and the attitudes behind them, because they were constructed years ago and have been a part of us for so long. They just seem, in our minds, to be who we are. In fact, sometimes when we sense something isn't quite right, we can direct all our efforts elsewhere, because to us our masks are an acceptable part of us. We don't even imagine that it is our masks that could be causing problems. I hope that, in the course of exploring further the reasons why we may wear masks, you will begin to recognize when your own personal mask-wearing is a hindrance to you enjoying all that God has for you as an individual.

Personal reflection

Spend some time reflecting on your own childhood. Here are some questions and ideas that you may find helpful:

- Do you recognize how your own inner critical voice mirrors the messages you were given in childhood?
- Ask God for revelation as to what patterns of your own behaviour have grown out of your childhood (both helpful and unhelpful).
- Do you recognize that you wear a particular mask in front of people? If not, could it be that you have simply accepted that it is a part of who you are? Do you think God could be nudging you to explore this idea further? If so, prayerfully ask for his guidance as you continue to work through the chapters.

Personality Types

As well as our upbringing impacting our behaviour, our own personalities can play a big part too. There are those of us who are naturally extroverted, who enjoy a lot of company and like the buzz of interaction. Others, myself included, are more introverted and can find large gatherings intimidating and off-putting (as I've already described). What is intriguing, however, is that both groups of people can believe that they *have* to be outgoing in order to be accepted. The result is that we can put on a mask and play a part for as long as we feel we need to. Let's explore why that is.

When looking at the definitions of the word 'mask' found in the dictionary, I discovered that they all include a sense of covering up – whether for amusement, protection or for disguising purposes. While we are going to be focusing on the more negative connotations of this, it is important to acknowledge that sometimes there is a positive result. Just like the image of masked people at a masquerade ball letting their hair down and acting out being another person, our masks can give us a sense of daring. In this instance, the pretending allows us to 'come out of ourselves'. When this happens, perhaps we engage with life in a way we would never otherwise do, and find a joy in doing so.

Masks can certainly be fun: I attended a friend's wedding a few years ago where there was a masked dance in the evening. Even though we could recognize one another, there was a sense of fun and frivolity that purely came out of the wearing of masks. Attending a masked ball again recently, this time with a close friend but mainly with people I'd only just met, the masks certainly helped to facilitate the relaxed atmosphere.

The flip side to all this, of course, is if we feel we *have* to play a part to be accepted in a particular setting, and it becomes a real strain to do so. As I have already indicated, as an introvert who occasionally battles with low self-esteem, I can put on a mask at times. I do it to make myself feel more presentable and like-able, and in order to convey the messages that I wish to. I talk to my nervous self sternly just before I speak publicly, to ensure it allows a more confident self to emerge. However, I am learn-ing that there is a big difference between stepping out of my natural comfort zone, relying on God's strength to accomplish something, and trying to 'fake it' by pretending to be someone I am not. The former leads to growth and humility – the latter, eventually, to unhelpful levels of stress (as we will explore later).

Feeling the pressure

The Latin word *persona* originally referred to a theatrical mask. It has been adopted by psychologists to describe the outer mask or façade that we present to others. There is a sense of it describing our public personalities, rather than the inner, true self. As someone who can actually sense myself closing down at times – and projecting an overly confident self at others – I wanted to explore how much of an impact our personalities have on our mask-wearing tendencies. Once again, I've found the studies undertaken by psychologists extremely helpful.

It was Carl Jung who first referred to this outwardly 'playing a part' as our 'persona', and he coined the terms 'introvert' and 'extrovert' too. In recent years, psychologists have argued about what exactly those terms mean, but nevertheless they still use them – and so do businesses and universities. (The Myers-Briggs personality test, for example, is based on Jung's thinking.) It can be helpful, for our own understanding of ourselves, to think about whether we have a particular bent towards one of these personality types.

As I mentioned, I see myself as more of an introvert. I love being with people, but can find small talk difficult and draining – particularly when talking to people I have just met. I feel inspired and invigorated when I have deep, honest conversations, but I still need space to rest and just 'be' afterwards, as it takes a lot out of me emotionally.[1] It has taken me a long time to realize that I need time to breathe and reflect, though, as I also suffer from the modern-day ailment of always being busy.

Author and speaker Michele Guinness spoke to me about how she is naturally an extrovert but can often feel that she is expected to behave in a certain way *all the time* because others recognize that in her too:

> There is one particular instance that has really stayed with me. Back when we lived in Nottingham, I was in a group setting where were doing an affirmation exercise, saying what we valued about each other. People all the way round said that they like my bubbliness, and I felt that no one had seen the real me in that group. Bubbliness does cheer people up, but I felt that I'm so much more than a bubble. I wondered, 'Is that just how people see me?'

People don't see the dark days. I can bounce back fairly quickly but there is a danger that if you are extrovert you are seen as the life and soul of the party; you are the 'up' one and you will carry the situation if everyone else dries up – so sometimes you feel that that's what you have to do. I love parties – but sometimes I feel like I have to take my persona with me.

There is an expectation on extroverts to fill all the gaps and carry situations but we don't always feel like it. Perhaps we carry our masks very close to us. I will say, 'I'm not feeling brilliant today,' but then flip it off with a joke so everyone feels okay. Extroverts are under an enormous pressure to please and make everyone else feel alright. We feel a pressure to make life easier for everyone.

I believe that both personality types can feel that pressure, because the extrovert is held up as the ideal within society.[2] We celebrate the self-starter, and expect those who get ahead in business or culture to be the ones who have the loudest voices and can take charge of others quickly and easily. But that isn't always the case.[3]

> The extrovert is held up as the ideal within society.

I have seen how this belief is being perpetuated within the younger generation through what happened to my daughter in the last few years of primary school. She is extremely similar to me and often behaves in a way that reminds me of myself at her age. She is painfully shy until she is in an environment where she feels comfortable. Very academically minded, she has had no problems with the levels of work at school and used to be very keen to answer her teachers' questions within class. But this changed when she had a male teacher for the first time. I was pleased, thinking it would be a good experience for her, but she found it uncomfortable and became shy all over again, and unfortunately his teaching style did nothing to help her overcome that. Parents' evenings were still full of praise but the comment that she needs to speak up more and share her ideas started to be made regularly.

I can see how difficult it is for her to speak up, especially when she sees those louder than her being listened to over and above herself. In the run up to a class assembly, she auditioned and got a part she loved, but then watched as the extrovert characters voiced what they wanted to do, and all of a sudden, her part was made smaller. I encouraged her to speak up and say what *she* wanted, but then I realized: here is a stark example of the extroverts being heard and an introvert being ignored. Surely in school everyone's strengths should be celebrated and nurtured in a safe environment? A class is going to be full of introverts as well as extroverts, so how teachers work at encouraging both is going to have a lasting legacy on those young lives.

Imposter syndrome

My husband Steve is also an introvert, but has experienced many situations in which he has been called upon to lead. This has, at times, caused him to struggle with the sense of not being qualified for the job. I asked him to reflect on how being an introvert has created conflict within himself:

> For most of my adult life I have been thrown in at the deep end leading people in many diverse areas; from helping to run a safari park in Tanzania at the tender age of eighteen, to recording and producing albums for many well-known artists, to leading a local church.

I have found I can be quite adaptable . . . and successful. However, I had a moment of self-discovery about a year ago (and for someone who doesn't usually process their emotional health, that is saying something). My discovery was that all these different areas of responsibility had left me feeling like a fake; feeling that one day my mask would be whipped off and I would be found out!

I have since discovered that I am not alone in feeling like this; in fact, it has a name – Imposter Syndrome. This was first identified by Dr Pauline R. Clance and Suzanne A. Imes in the 1970s. Being an introvert by nature, and yet being very adept at 'acting' the extrovert leader, had left me feeling that my successes were down to this act.

Since discovering this trait in my thinking, I have been able to realize that, far from being an act, God had enabled me, and still does, to be adaptable and flourish in different situations. I have discovered that regularly stepping into uncomfortable territory is God's way of stretching us and making sure we rely on him. I have also been learning to be secure in who God made me to be. This is something I can thank him for and celebrate, rather than feel any sense of hypocrisy over.

The stress we can put our bodies under

I can relate so much to what Steve says about stepping out as an introvert, because it reflects my own experience. There was much I didn't quite understand about extroverts, until I started reading around the subject. I had always assumed extroverts are extremely comfortable within social settings, and I longed to be more like them. But, when reading *The Human Face of Church*, I first came across what psychologist Dorothy Rowe believes is the untold stress for extroverts:

that being rejected by a group of people has such an immense effect on an extrovert their very sense of self can be threatened by it.[4] This means that an extrovert can 'play to the crowd' as it were, becoming what they believe people want from them (which, as we have seen, Michele admitted she can feel the pressure to do).

Interestingly, a lot of artistic types, including actors, musicians and writers, are, by their very nature, introverts – it's what gives them the impetus to create while alone. And yet they have to publicize their work and so they 'become' more extrovert in order to market themselves (and obviously performers enjoy being on a stage for a time). In a way, they need to wear the mask of behaving like an extrovert. But of course, things are never that simple, and we can't compartmentalize people neatly with labels.

In a seminar I attended a few years ago, Revd Will van der Hart, speaking about creative personality types, suggested that, for them, living authentically can often mean living with both extrovert and introvert selves.[5] He believes that, rather than being one or the other, everyone may have tendencies for both, depending on the situation. I found that profound, and accept that there are times that many of us do need to embrace either our more extrovert or introvert side. However, I do think most of us are predominantly one or the other and that sometimes, to fit into a particular situation, we wear a mask that takes real effort, as it isn't who we really are.

I don't think that there is necessarily anything wrong with pushing ourselves outside our comfort zones (as we've seen, it is a key way that we can grow). However, it is good to understand the type of person that we are, as by wearing a mask that isn't our true self for too long, we are putting ourselves under incredible strain. We can get to the point that triggers our body's natural 'fight or flight' instinct. This is an automatic response that our bodies make to a potentially dangerous situation – and it gives the same physical response whether that danger is physical or emotional:

> By wearing a mask that isn't our true self for too long, we are putting ourselves under incredible strain.

What is actually happening is the brain is picking up a potential crisis and is preparing the body to either fight the perceived threat or run away from it (take flight). This is obviously essential in life-threatening situations when, perhaps, oncoming traffic suddenly swerves towards you. When our self-preservation instincts kick in it will ensure that our responses are quicker in order to protect ourselves from danger. However when we experience a threat to our self-image or someone insists on their own way, we can become very angry because the 'fight or flight' has responded to the threat to our personhood. Our bodies can't automatically differentiate between what is an objective threat and what is a subjective one.[6]

Our fight or flight response can kick in when we are in a stressful situation, such as a big social gathering that we are uncomfortable in. Perhaps, for example, we have been 'encouraged' to speak up and all eyes are suddenly on us. Our hearts usually start to beat faster when that happens. But the resulting rapid release of adrenaline and the effect that has on our bodies means that it isn't healthy to stay in such a situation for too long. The automatic fight-or-flight instinct puts our bodies on high alert. Our hearts race, our pupils enlarge, our muscles tense, our breathing deepens, our hands can go clammy – basically, we are put under huge tension. Ultimately, that's going to have a negative effect on our physical (and emotional) wellbeing.

I have certainly felt all the physical effects that are described above, and it makes sense that interacting with others in a way that isn't so natural for us is going to leave a lasting impact on us. When we can recognize and understand our personality type, and the situations that may call for us to operate outside of our natural comfort zone, we can keep tabs on the level of stress we are encountering from this. It is worth remembering that while our instinct may be to reach for our masks in an effort to protect ourselves, by the very act of doing so, we may be doing the exact opposite by causing our bodies to be put under intense pressure. Learning to embrace who we are can help us to avoid feeling that we always need to push ourselves to respond in a particular way. We do need to be aware of when the Holy Spirit (rather than our culture) prompts us to step out of our comfort zones, but God made each of us individuals with different personalities, so let's celebrate that.

Personal reflection

- Reflect on how your personality type affects the way that you interact with others.
- What situations cause you to feel under stress? How can you manage those more effectively? Do you need to ensure that you aren't putting yourself into so many of those situations?
- Spend some time reflecting on the fact that God made you, knows your personality and accepts you completely. Rest in this total acceptance and love for a few moments.

Influenced by Our Culture

Western culture is so busy, and so full of influences – be it the media, technology that we interact with daily or simply the schedules that our workplaces demand we fit into. I have already mentioned that our culture celebrates extroverts, and that even our children are measured by performance.

As I have been thinking about the effect this all has upon us, I have noticed more and more that everything we see around us perpetuates the need to be 'successful' and 'look the part'. This can, again, have us reaching for our masks if we don't feel we measure up. We are constantly being sent messages about what we should look like, what it means to be a success – and what things we should own in order to enjoy our lives to the full.[1]

Billboards, magazines, websites and TV, for example, all show us what they think constitutes beauty – and yet so often it isn't real or healthy. Models are instructed to stick to a rigid weight, celebrity pictures in magazines are photoshopped, and some women resort to facelifts, tummy tucks and breast enhancements to desperately try to hide the effects of ageing.

It wasn't that long ago that my son watched me frantically applying make-up before going on the school run. He looked up and asked, so simply and innocently, 'Mummy why do you wear make-up?' The question cut me to the quick. I realized that I use cosmetics to feel more confident, to cover over those parts of my face that I don't like as much these days because there are lines (and often dark circles). But it has made me question what message I am giving to my daughter, who loves playing around with make-up (having older cousins she looks up to and tries to imitate). I've admitted to her that I feel a certain level of pressure to mask over the ageing parts of me, because they don't seem so acceptable now – especially when I compare myself to other mums who still look so young and natural![2]

The same is true of my body: I can see I've put on weight in the last few years since passing the big 4-0 landmark. I don't like the extra weight I'm carrying, but I'm trying very hard not to make a big deal out of it, as I simply don't want to be that mum who asks constantly, 'Does my bum look big in this?' (Partly because I know my son is very honest and will tell me when it does!) Sometimes I do fail, such as the day my daughter and I went on a girly shopping trip with some money we had earned together reviewing a book for a magazine. She found a pair of jeans that fitted her so well. I looked at her svelte, pert body and everything I tried on after that moment made me feel fat and frumpy. I came away mightily fed up, and without a purchase of my own. I felt the need to hide under baggy clothes so that people couldn't really see me.

But why do I feel fat and old? I am not overweight, and have not reached old age yet. It is, partly, I believe, because my culture has told me that it is the young and beautiful who are desirable. I've explained to my daughter that I know when I am influenced in such a way it is unhelpful – and unnecessary; that I try to remember to take those feelings of not measuring up to

God and ask him to remind me that I'm loved and accepted by him. While I need to look after my body, I do not need to be a slave to it. I don't want her to struggle in the same way as I have – but, unfortunately, I know so many women do and a lot of it is down to the messages we receive.

It isn't just women, either. Men, too, are encouraged to work on their pecs until they are as rock solid as the six-packs that adorn the male models' bodies on the front of men's magazines. The male grooming industry is now huge, bringing in multiple billions of pounds annually.[3] Society calls it 'progress', as men are now making an effort with their outward appearance . . .

We receive messages about other aspects of life, too. We watch programmes portraying highly successful business people at the top of their game – whatever that is – and wonder why we aren't doing as well as them. Workplace culture can demand we put in so many hours that we have little time left to be refreshed. In such an unhealthy, comparison-driven environment it can be hard not to let the striving syndrome rub off on us – whether inside or outside of church. I know that hearing about women who manage to juggle amazing careers as well as motherhood with seeming ease can make me feel inadequate. It also fuels my inner craving for the same levels of achievement.

> In such an unhealthy, comparison-driven environment it can be hard not to let the striving syndrome rub off on us.

When we are describing ourselves to someone new, we often focus on our achievements rather than our struggles – perhaps even over-emphasizing those achievements a little to seem as successful as we can.

Social media's 'sting'

There is one thing that is now embedded in our culture, but which has had an extraordinarily rapid rise. When I was a child, the internet simply did not exist – now children seem to be born with an inherent knowledge of how to use it. But what effect has the social media phenomenon the internet has spawned had on our sense of self? A couple of decades ago no one would have dreamed of sharing photos of every significant moment of their – and their family's – life. Yet now so many people do it at a touch of a button, without even thinking. Why is that?

I think one of the reasons social media has become so widely used is because it is *such* an easy way for people to connect with lots of others. We all crave friendship; I have enjoyed catching up with friends I had when I lived in America when I was 8 years old. It's incredible how these networks can facilitate long-distance reunions.

As well as connecting with friends, we use it to learn and talk about a whole range of subjects that were taboo back in our grandparents' day, but that cultural openness hasn't necessarily created truly open and honest relationships. Certainly we no longer have what society would view as the tight-lipped approach of the past, but has technology freed us or actually made us wear our masks more tightly?

> Has technology freed us or actually made us wear our masks more tightly?

Take Facebook for instance. People's statuses usually go one of two ways: a post about how wonderful life is (something they or a family member has achieved) or a really negative post about how rubbish life is (usually accompanied by lots of sympathetic comments). We can forget that Facebook is an incomplete snap-shot of true life. Even if it looks like we are gaining great insights, it is actually a skewed view.

Why do people love to 'share' their most successful moments on social media? Because, so often, their success 'needs' to be measured by how others respond to it. And that's due to our inbuilt need for acceptance and recognition again. We all have those needs, and it is natural to want people to acknowledge when we've achieved something. We long for those around us to praise us for it.

I have a sneaking suspicion, however, that social media also has a sting in its tail. While people share more online it can sometimes be fairly superficial and 'man-aged'. We ensure those viewing our posts see the bit of us that we want them to see.

> Social media perpetuates the mask-wearing syndrome.

So, by its very nature, social media perpetuates the mask-wear-ing syndrome. We get so used to 'managing our image' – it be-comes almost automatic. It can even cause us to continue to do so when we interact with others face to face too. This is by no means a new tendency, but social media has certainly in-creased it.

Here are some of the thoughts from respondents of my sur-vey on how social media use can affect us:

'People seem to expose themselves too much on social media and hide when they come to church!'

'We share our edited life, the good bits. When you're having a bad day seeing someone's good day can make you feel inadequate.'

'My impression is that people tend to be positive and witty on so-cial media rather than real.'

'Social media is the best platform to enable one to wear a mask. You are in control of what you put out there, so you only reveal what you want to reveal.'

'We can unconsciously present ourselves as an avatar – how we wish ourselves to be seen, not as we actually are.'

'We seem to have entered into a culture of constantly wanting to seek approval and social media provides that platform.'

'It appears that people on social media share what they wish their lives were, not what their lives actually are.'

'My Facebook is positive and doesn't reveal the real me.'

'I lead a Beach Mission every year. One team member was anxious about approaching me because I'd had such an amazing year (on Facebook). She was shocked to hear how low I had got that year.'

The truth is, people often expect us to be like the image we portray on social media. Depending on our use of such platforms, that can create a real pressure – and a distortion of the truth of who we really are.

Please don't misunderstand me. I can see the positives of connectivity that social media can provide. And sometimes it actually *helps* people to open up about their struggles in a way they wouldn't feel comfortable doing face to face with someone. It is wonderful when they are able to find help as a result. But I do believe social media can also have a negative impact. We post something on Facebook and expect a response. If we don't get it we feel let down – or think that the problem must be with us, so we start to think negatively about ourselves. I have certainly done that myself.

A study of around 600 adults in Germany undertaken in 2013 revealed that interaction on Facebook has produced a basis for comparison and envy on a scale never before seen.[4] Around a third of those participating said they felt mainly negative feelings when using Facebook. The research concluded that the main cause of those feelings was down to envy.

Chine Mbubaegbu, author of *Am I Beautiful?*[5] told me that she recognizes the effects Facebook statuses can have on herself and others:

> Social media exacerbates an underlying propensity that so many of us have to want what other people have. It's rare to feel content in our status, our situations, our characters. So many of us tie ourselves up in knots with this lack of contentment and this all-consuming comparison. Although social media sites can be such a force for good, we need to see them for what they are – ways that all of us use to make our lives seem so much more put-together than they really are.

When we try to create a positive spin in our everyday lives online, we are in fact creating an artificial bubble that can become unhealthy, especially if it seeps into the rest of life.

After a crisis in her marriage, and a life-changing decision to move (leaving her career behind) Esther Emery decided that she needed to take a complete break from using social media. Her book *What Falls From the Sky* charts her year away from the internet.[6] It was a year that helped her reconnect with God, but also taught her a lot about why she had been chasing after success and what really mattered in life:

As long as I was on the internet, my value and worth was up for discussion. And the more fragile I got, because of the crisis in my marriage and the loss of my career, the more I cared. When I dropped off the internet I was running away from all of that. And also, somewhere deep inside, I was running towards hope. I felt hope that if I could just rest a little, I could make things better, and that's in fact exactly how it turned out.

I learned how to be who I am when nobody is watching. I learned that I am still a person – still a person of value – even when I'm not producing anything particularly useful. I learned that silence heals. And silence is essentially – practically – synonymous with the presence of God. The way I see it, we have a kind of reset button in our souls. You can always go back to the beginning and be contrite and be grateful, and you really do get another chance. But it takes such courage and humility to keep going back to that. Sometimes the only way is to step into a place completely without mirrors, with nothing to distract or stroke the ego, so the strongest pull becomes the pull to what is right, which is always returning to the presence of God, the silence and the still small voice.

God's view of success

While our culture may have its specific ideas about what constitutes success, God has his own and it is very simple, as Esther discovered. It is faithfulness. Church leader John Lanferman unpacked this further at a recent conference I attended, reminding us that the one thing common to all those listed in the hall of fame within Hebrews 11 is faith. Each new person in that chapter is introduced with the phrase 'by faith'. And many of the things they did by faith would not have been seen as successful by those around them. Think of Noah and how he must have been ridiculed when he faithfully built the ark as he was instructed to – before the rain had even begun. Certainly no one else was expecting the deluge that caused the flood (see Gen. 6).

God doesn't ask anything more of us than to be faithful with what he has given us, and what he has called us to. It's great to remind ourselves of that regularly, especially when we can sense we are really feeling the pressure to be 'successful' in the world's eyes.

Personal reflection

- Are there parts of your character or appearance that you find difficult to accept? If so, why do you think that is?
- How do you think that you are influenced by the messages (social) media portray about what you should look like and/or what it means to be a success? Could this have happened subconsciously?
- Take some time before God, asking him to forgive you for the times when you've allowed culture to shape you, rather than his Word. Ask him to help you be more alert to the messages that society constantly feeds you, and to learn to reject those that do not line up with what he says about you.

Fear of What Others Think

Perhaps unsurprisingly, fear of others' perceptions of us topped my survey. This is an area that seems able to paralyse us wherever we are. In church, we can perhaps look around and, instead of being encouraged by being among other Christians, only see how amazing everyone else looks and how well their lives seem to be going. That makes us feel worse about ourselves before we've even spent five minutes in the building. To blend in, we desperately cover over our difficulties and struggles, as we don't want people to think badly of us.

> To blend in, we desperately cover over our difficulties and struggles, as we don't want people to think badly of us.

I don't know if you've ever done that – but I certainly have, time and time again. I am humbled now when I think of it, as the Pharisees spring to mind. And Jesus had some pretty harsh things to say about them. In Matthew 23, he warned the people about how the Pharisees puffed themselves up and liked to look important. They were all about the outer appearance, with little substance inside. He went on to condemn their actions directly with phrases all beginning with 'Woe to you' (see verses 13–32). Jesus always got to the heart of the matter, and was angered and frustrated by the hypocrisy of the religious leadership of his day.

Jesus actually called the Pharisees hypocrites directly to their faces – quite a few times (see vv.13, 15, 23, 25, 27, 29). The word hypocrite comes from the Greek *hypokrité*, which means stage player or pretender. It was used to refer to a travelling actor, who often wore a mask to help project the sense of who he was supposed to be. So, by comparing the Pharisees to such a person, Jesus was saying that they were putting on an act, pretending to be holy.

The Pharisees' position was reliant on them being able to keep the Law. They thought God's approval was based on their performance. Can we, too, believe that to a certain extent? Do we think our acceptability to God is based on our performance? Does this make us afraid to show weakness to others?

I do think this can be a subconscious reasoning that affects our behaviour. It can, unfortunately, make us more interested in how we are perceived by those around us than in making sure our hearts stay soft and humble. We can also judge others by their outer appearances rather than their inner lives.

I know that many times I have made assumptions simply on what someone looked like outwardly and tried to match the positive persona I thought I was seeing. I compared myself to them, feeling like I was the only struggling one as a result, and didn't want others to see my weakness in case it changed their opinion of me. So I put on an act in an effort to live up to what I thought they were. It took me a long time to understand that by comparing myself to whichever person it was, I was comparing all my week's baggage with their present image – and often I did it without even speaking to them!

God gently began to talk to me and remind me that what I was seeing on the outside was just a snapshot of their life. I couldn't possibly know what their week had been like and how they were emotionally, physically and spiritually, without asking them – and without them giving an honest answer. So to base my response to people on so many assumptions was really unhealthy and unhelpful.

Longing for connection

The truth is, many of us are longing to know that we are not alone in our struggles. One of the wonderful things about church is that we can meet like-minded people and learn to support one another. Sometimes as a pastor's wife, I can feel quite isolated, as there are very few people that truly understand the particular pressures within our lives. But I was recently reminded of the joy of connecting with someone who shares the same life experiences as me.

I was attending a course, and at the end of the evening meal I happened to go up to the hot-drinks table at the same time as another woman who is a pastor's wife. After the initial pleasantries of 'How are you?' and 'How has your month been?' it was as if we both gave each other silent permission to share more deeply. Suddenly, there was a torrent of words flowing from both of us, and lots of 'Me too!' exclamations. We had opened up and discovered shared experiences, and just knowing there was someone who truly understood was so good for my soul.

> Spending time with another who is happy to share openly who they are, encourages us, and we are able to respond in kind.

I came away from that particular encounter incredibly encouraged. I reflected on how spending time with another who is happy to share openly who they are – who they *really* are – encourages us, and we are able to respond in kind. That friend was not afraid of telling me what she was going through, and it enabled me to do the same. The supportive remarks, encouragements and words of wisdom that were shared did us both so much good.

The sad thing is often we don't get past the 'How are you?' and 'I am fine' brief conversation. While we may be pressed for time at the start of a meeting, or we are talking to someone we don't know that well so don't feel comfortable opening up further, too often it is the assumptions and comparisons that stop us from sharing with anyone more deeply.

The wrong source

Why is it that we seem so desperate to be liked by those around us? The Bible reveals to us how much we are loved by God, but often that doesn't seem to be enough for us.

In fact, every so often I ask myself: is God enough for me?

I know the spiritual answer to that – of course he is! In fact, it seems like a terrible oxymoron. How could I even ask such a question? But I do it regularly because I know I need to check whether I am actually living like I believe that he is.

I have a feeling we can struggle in this area because we need something tangible, right in front of us. It reminds me once again of my angry response to God when he said he would be my husband. I couldn't reach out and touch him and so I rejected his attempts to draw me closer to him. Sadly, I think we can often look to

> We can often look to something physical rather than spiritual to meet our deep inner needs.

something physical rather than spiritual to meet our deep inner needs. It could be because that seems to be a more immediate answer to our problems – but usually it doesn't last.

This isn't a recent phenomenon – a look at the nation God called his own, Israel, shows us that they often turned to other things to feed their needs, even building idols that they thought would help them with this. In Jeremiah God says: 'My people have exchanged their glorious God for worthless idols . . . My people have committed two sins: They have forsaken me, the spring of living water, and have dug their own cisterns, broken cisterns that cannot hold water' (Jer. 2:11,13).

We can read through their story and judge them as being fickle. He was so evidently with them, and did some amazing miracles for them, and yet they seemed to forget those so quickly and wander away from him. And yet, with our similar inner longings for acceptance and love we can do exactly the same by looking to other sources than God. His living water is the only one that can completely satisfy – and will never run dry – and yet we still look to other things, including the acceptance of those around us. While hankering after this, we put up 'fronts' to make ourselves look as much like the sort of people we think others want us to be as possible.

The Bible tells us that 'perfect love drives out fear' (1 John 4:18). God is perfect love – and it is his enemy that loves to keep us trapped behind our masks out of fear. If he can make us believe that people will think badly of us if we are truly ourselves then he can ensure that God's community isn't functioning as it should. So he thinks it is fantastic when we believe his lies. More often than not, he does a great job of just dropping the idea into our heads that people would be offended by the real us. We then pick it up and start to believe it. I am convinced that a lot of the battle in this area is in our mind, and so I explore the concept of 'renewing our minds' in Chapter 14.

Known and accepted by the one who really matters

The ironic thing is that we can spend so much time carefully manufacturing the way we are perceived by those around us, to gain their approval and acceptance, that we forget that God knows absolutely everything about us and accepts us anyway. He knows our thoughts and the words we are going to say:

> You have searched me, LORD,
>   and you know me.
> You know when I sit and when I rise;
>   you perceive my thoughts from afar.
> You discern my going out and my lying down;
>   you are familiar with all my ways.
> Before a word is on my tongue
>   you, LORD, know it completely (Ps. 139:1–4).

That is quite a difficult concept to fully grasp – the psalmist even said, 'Such knowledge is too wonderful for me, too lofty for me to attain' (v.6). And yet, the truth is, God knows us through and through. While we may fear the unknown judgement of those around us, wondering what they will think of us if we open up to them, God's judgement is already in. Through Jesus' sacrifice and our repentance we are able to be recipients of his acceptance, love, compassion, grace and mercy.

What's our view of God?

Sometimes I think we can place an over-emphasis on wanting to be loved and accepted by those around us, because we have a wrong view of God. This stops us from entering into the full relationship he offers us, stops us from seeking after his friendship and opinion more than anyone else's.

For example, we may have had a particular aspect of his character emphasized to us as we grew up, or in the teaching of our church, and that has caused us to have a distorted picture of who he is. While what we believe may be true, when it is the only, or main, view we have of him we miss out on the full picture.

Many of us view God as creator, but if that is the main, or only, view we have of him he can seem somewhat impersonal – a force that works in the distance rather than longing for intimacy with us. What about God as provider? We love to remind one another of that amazing aspect of his character and yet, if that is the part of him that we think about most, we can view him as there specifically for our benefit. It can cause us to be totally disillusioned when he doesn't do what we expect or want him to.

If we view God mainly as Lord, someone to be honoured and obeyed, we can become so focused on rules and obligations that we miss the message of God's grace. One aspect that I think the modern evangelical church has had a tendency to over-emphasize, particularly in its songs, is God as our friend. It is true that he is, but this can cause us to view him too casually. We can lose the necessary sense of awe and wonder that would help us to cultivate a reverential fear that would mean we care more about God's opinion than others'.

Of course, the devil loves to distort the truth of who God is, even just a little bit, in order to throw us off balance. We see how he did it with Eve, getting her to question what God said, and ultimately leading her to disobedience – which resulted in broken relationship.

It is so vital that we immerse ourselves in Scripture, so that we get a true and bigger picture about who God is. He is so incredible, so awe-inspiring, that we will never run out of new things to discover about him. God also goes to great lengths, sometimes through our difficulties, to point out our wrong views of who he is, because he knows they can be a hindrance to us discovering the depths of his love for us. It was out of love that he sent Jesus to the earth, and it is what Jesus reveals to us that is the most vital part of God's character towards us. Understanding this is what moves our head knowledge of who God is into a heart knowledge that cultivates a thriving, loving relationship between God and us.

Our Father

Everything that Jesus did while he walked on earth was for one purpose: to restore us into right relationship with the Father. When he conversed with God, and when he described him to others, he used the name Father more than anything else. He revealed to humanity that God, ultimately, is our Father and longs for relationship with us. We might have allowed ourselves to fixate on what other people think of us – but God offers us unconditional acceptance and love! When we allow ourselves to dive into that love, what other people think of us becomes much less important because we have found the one who absolutely and totally loves the real us.

Exploring the father heart of God brings great freedom to many. Just a quick search online will show you that there is a wealth of courses that focus on this (and if this is something you have never explored, attending a course could be extremely helpful).

I do understand that for some, the images produced by the word 'father' are not positive, as their experience with their earthly father was painful and difficult. It can cause a projection of the hurt from that kind of father onto God, which stifles the ability to feel a connection with him. I can't pretend to understand that fully, but I do know, coming from a background where my parents divorced and my mother remarried when I was young, that I reached my teenage years thoroughly confused about fatherhood.

As I mentioned, I have a very loving stepfather, who I relate to as my dad. He has been there for me through everything and given me a stable and loving upbringing. He has loved me unconditionally and has been an amazing father, helping me to feel safe and secure. While we moved around every few years for his work, when my sister and I started secondary school, we settled in one place so that our exam preparation would not be disrupted. Our new location happened to be much nearer to my biological father. This meant we began to see him more regularly.

I became very conscious of not wanting to upset either of my dads, and of trying to understand why I found it difficult to relate to my biological dad. In my mid-teens I hit a crisis point about this issue. I was so churned up inside. It was then that God gently spoke to me, inviting me to lay down my anxieties and rest in him. He asked me to allow him to reveal to me how he is my perfect, heavenly Father and that I do not need to worry about trying to sort out everything else in my head. He poured such peace into my troubled soul, and the knowledge that reached deep down into my heart that day has brought such comfort over the years.

My friend Louise courageously admits that she allowed her understanding of fatherhood to colour her experiences with God for many years:

> My parents split up when I was five. I didn't see my dad much and I was desperate to be noticed by him. My relationship with him impacted my understanding of my relationship with God the Father. I set out on the same journey I had with my dad – I had to do all I could to make God proud of me. It was something I was convinced that I needed to work hard to achieve. But my relationship with my dad also played a big part in keeping me hidden and quiet. If my earthly father didn't want me, then what hope did I have?
>
> God has gently and graciously taught me to accept that I am his child – and that I don't need to do anything to earn his love. And as I have now fully accepted him as my Father it has given me the ability to forgive and release the expectations I put on my earthly father. I am now free from finding my identity in him. I have also reconciled with him.

It may be that your experience of fatherhood on earth has not been positive; while we are never asked to simply dismiss the difficulties of the past, each of us is invited to meditate on the amazing truth that we have been adopted by a gracious, all-knowing and all-loving Father (see 1 John 3:1, Rom. 8:14–17).

God wants to gently remind you that your experiences do not change his character. He treasures you in a way that no one on earth can and longs to be the one who matters most to you.

We can sometimes question the truth of that, especially when verses such as '"For I know the plans I have for you," declares the LORD, "plans to prosper you and not to harm you, plans to give you hope and a future"' (Jer. 29:11) seem to fly in the face of what we are currently experiencing. Too often that verse is used to tell us that we should be expecting prosperity and wealth in our lives, so when we don't experience them it leaves us questioning God's goodness.

I found it so interesting to discover recently that the original word for plans is *machashabah*, which literally means 'thoughts'.[1] So God knows the thoughts he has towards us – and they are *always* loving and good. Someone else's opinion of me need not define who I am, especially when I can rest in the knowledge that my God always looks towards me with thoughts of love.

> Someone else's opinion of me need not define who I am.

An audience of one

I have heard many preachers and worship leaders speak about living for 'an audience of one'. I find it a really helpful reminder to me that my focus should be on what God thinks of me, rather than what others think. Knowing that he loves me unconditionally gives me the fuel to help me serve him, even in the midst of difficulties – and even when those around me misunderstand me.

I find it encouraging to remind myself of those who did this well in the Bible. I think of people like Mordecai, who refused to bow down to Haman (see Esth. 3) because it would be dishonouring to God. Daniel, too, had the courage to speak out the interpretation of the writing on the wall that appeared before King Belshazzar, even though it was not a positive message. He also refused to bow down and worship King Darius (see Dan. 6). These courageous men had their eyes fixed on God and sought true validation, love and acceptance from him alone. They didn't give weight to other people's opinions of them (both had men seeking to discredit them for being who they were), and didn't bow down to the pressure to conform. I know that I don't always get that right, but I long for that to be something that can be said of me too.

Personal reflection

- Take some time to ask yourself whether God is enough for you. Be honest! (It may be helpful to reflect on whether you have a tendency to look to the physical rather than spiritual to meet your inner needs as you do this.)
- Do you struggle to accept that God loves you as you are? If so, perhaps you could ask him to help you open yourself up more fully to his love right now?
- What does the image of God as Father conjure up in your mind? If your own experiences of fatherhood have been negative, could you take some time to bring them before God now in prayer, asking him to help you understand that he is your perfect father? You may well need to spend some time working through the issues you have experienced with your earthly father. Asking God for support with that, as well as a trusted friend and/or counsellor perhaps, could be the next step for you.

Fear of Rejection

For some of us, there is an overwhelming fear of revealing who we really are because we believe we will be rejected if we do so. This may be due to hurtful past experiences in either childhood or adulthood, or it could be unfounded fear. Whichever it is, it has a *huge* influence on the way we interact with those in church. As Russell Willingham says in his book *Relational Masks*, 'What death is to the body, abandonment is to the soul.'[1]

Recent research shows the emotional pain of rejection registers in the same part of our brain as physical pain.[2] Our response is similar too – we try to avoid the pain at all costs. And so our masks become our way of trying to ensure we are protected from emotional pain.

For example, we can find ourselves trying to blend in with whatever those around us are doing and saying, just so we don't make ourselves stand out. We may avoid arguments of any kind, and listen intently to what other people are saying so that we don't say anything that we think will be unpopular.

Sometimes this is why we are afraid to be honest about our struggles, temptations and sins. Confessing our sins to one another leads to freedom and support, but too often we shrink back from that level of openness, worried about what people's response will be (as we looked at in the last chapter). The trouble is, so many of us are scared of rejection that it is a self-perpetuating cycle.

As we saw in the last chapter, if we say to ourselves, 'If people really knew me they wouldn't love me', we are actually believing a lie that comes directly from the devil. Sometimes he even encourages us to wear our masks and then winds us up further by whispering the idea that people can still see through us, can still see our faults. (This is something I intimated in the introduction. While I felt I had been put on a pedestal of sorts by others, I still thought – even with all my efforts to hide it – that they must have been able to see the real, hurting me underneath.) Such lies can cause us to hold our masks even tighter. But by keeping our masks up for fear of rejection, we are asking others to love unreality. People cannot truly love us until they know who we really are.

> People cannot truly love us until they know who we really are.

The devil loves for us to be fearful, so feeds us yet another lie: that we are the only one with this issue. The fact is, so many of us struggle with this – something we would quickly discover if we were to take that step of being honest with those around us.

My friend Louise explained to me that she had been addicted to the approval of others for years. The fear of being rejected made her try to be all things to all people, which ultimately was exhausting. It began back in her childhood, but continued to affect her relationships once she was an adult too – including those within church:

As I said previously, my parents separated when I was 5, and from that point on I lived my life to gain the approval of my dad. Every decision I made, every move that I made was all motivated by a desperation to hear the words 'I'm proud of you'. The emptiness I was so desperate to fill led to me looking for approval from everyone as I grew older. I had to do better, be better.

It was all about achievement and doing, and nothing about being myself. In fact, the more I fell into this trap, the more of myself was lost and buried deep behind the mask of service, of doing good, of saying yes, of helping, of being the go-to person.

Behind the scenes, I was often exhausted, miserable and struggling. I knew that I wasn't being myself but the person I was, as far as I was concerned, no one wanted to see or hear.

For years, the real me was voiceless. It was easier to hide behind my mask, as I was gripped with fear that I couldn't truly be known by anyone and accepted. God has taken me on a huge journey over the last few years, enabling me to recognize that I am his child and can simply accept his love rather than having to strive for it. This has enabled me to become secure in my identity. It has also given me the confidence to use the voice that had been quiet for so many years. I realized that people wanted to listen and that I had things to say. There was a real sense of freedom in being me, just as I am and not having to have a persona, or pretend.

Far from being scary, being real was actually a relief. There was no longer a narrative running in my head – telling me not to do that or say that. I have been able to develop open and honest relationships with others and share all that I am.

I love the extract from *The Velveteen Rabbit* that follows, as it reflects how time and life experiences (both good and painful) shape us, but that, if we have the courage to be 'real' about who we are, we become beautiful. It is only those who don't understand who we truly are, who perhaps don't take the time to find out, that can't see that beauty. The message of this story is that there is value in being real – something that Louise discovered for herself in her journey.

'What is REAL?' asked the Rabbit one day, when they were lying side by side near the nursery fender, before Nana came to tidy the room. 'Does it mean having things that buzz inside you and a stick-out handle?'

'Real isn't how you are made,' said the Skin Horse. 'It's a thing that happens to you. When a child loves you for a long, long time, not just to play with, but REALLY loves you, then you become Real.'

'Does it hurt?' asked the Rabbit.

'Sometimes,' said the Skin Horse, for he was always truthful. 'When you are Real you don't mind being hurt.'

'Does it happen all at once, like being wound up,' he asked, 'or bit by bit?'

'It doesn't happen all at once,' said the Skin Horse. 'You become. It takes a long time. That's why it doesn't happen often to people who break easily, or have sharp edges, or who have to be carefully kept. Generally, by the time you are Real, most of your hair has been loved off, and your eyes drop out and you get loose in the joints and very shabby. But these things don't matter at all, because once you are Real you can't be ugly, except to people who don't understand.'[3]

Have we rejected others?

I found it a really interesting exercise, when thinking about being rejected, to also think about whether I have rejected anyone else within church – knowingly or unknowingly. Doing this helped me see behind the rejection to the core reasons for it. Too often we can reject others out of fear. We aren't sure how to help or deal with the person that we have just been confronted with, so our response is to run and hide. Perhaps what they are going through is so far removed from our own situation that we don't know how to reach out to them. Or perhaps we don't feel we have the theological knowledge to give them helpful advice or support them well and so we keep them at arm's length. But have we considered the message that that gives to the other person? Sometimes all they need is a listening ear – they aren't always looking for an answer from us, simply empathy.

God tells us that 'all have sinned and fall short of the glory of God' (Rom. 3:23) and we are also given a stark warning by Jesus that we have no right to judge another human being: 'Do not judge, or you too will be judged. For in the same way as you judge others, you will be judged, and with the measure you use, it will be measured to you' (Matt. 7:1–2). Ouch. God has been talking to me recently about humility, and I know part of that is recognizing the times when I have the tendency to see the speck in a brother's or sister's eye while ignoring the plank in mine.

The good news is that, while we are all sinners, Jesus came to set us free: 'all are justified freely by his grace through the redemption that came by Christ Jesus' (Rom. 3:24).

Not giving up

If people have rejected us in the past, even if we know and fully accept the good news of what Jesus has done for us, the experience can colour the way that we interact with others. We may experience a similar rejection in the workplace, but when it happens at the hands of fellow Christians we can find it more

difficult to deal with. This could be because, while we may expect to be mistreated by other people, we don't expect it from
Christians and so are shocked when it happens. But this can
cause us to put up walls and wear masks, to ensure we don't
allow ourselves to be rejected by anyone in church in the present or future. However, it is important for us not to give up on
church as a whole when someone, or a group of people, hurts
us. Church is God's idea for community – and for reaching the
world. While we are all imperfect and so may hurt one another
at times, he actively encourages us to fellowship with one another regularly. Indeed, in Hebrews 10 Paul writes: 'Let us . . . not
give up meeting together' (vv.24–5).

It may feel like going it alone with God is much more appealing – but a solitary Christian is much more vulnerable to
attack, and to being tricked by the devil (and our own minds)
into believing things that aren't true. I remember reading
about author and theologian Philip Yancey's own journey with
this in his book *What's so Amazing About Grace?*[4] He talked
about turning away from church because he thought it was so
graceless, only to return after a time because he couldn't find
grace anywhere else – however hard he looked.

If you have experienced rejection from others in church,
I don't want to make any over simplified suggestions –
but I also don't want you to be stuck in the pain of rejection. Can
I gently suggest that you ask God to help you take the pain to
him as a starting point? As Psalm 50:15 says: 'Call on me in the
day of trouble'. Ask him to work in your heart, healing the pain
and also helping you to release your feelings towards the other
person (or people). Forgiveness plays a vital part in us being
able to experience God's healing and walk free from emotional
pain. In the chapter on disappointment, I talk about how God

first taught me about that – and also look in more depth about how we can learn to let go of disappointment and other hurts.

Never rejected by God

Being rejected can also cause us to become bitter towards God, as we feel he shouldn't have allowed any of his children to act in such a way towards us. However, it is important that we don't blame God for what other people have done. Because the truth is, he never rejects us. Here are some Scriptures that remind us of that:

> 'Never will I leave you; never will I forsake you' (Heb. 13:5. See also Deut. 31:6).
>
> 'Surely I am with you always, to the very end of the age' (Matt. 28:20).
>
> 'I have loved you with an everlasting love; I have drawn you with unfailing kindness' (Jer. 31:3).

I love that last verse in particular; it is littered throughout my journal as it has spoken to me deeply over the years. I have also been hugely impacted by the story of Joseph (which can be found in Gen. 37; 39–47). He was totally rejected by his family – left for dead by jealous brothers. Even the ones whose hearts were softer towards him did little; while Reuben stopped his brothers from killing Joseph, his suggestion of throwing him in a cistern with the idea of returning later revealed his cowardice in front of his brothers – see Genesis 37:19–30. Joseph was sold into slavery, but we are told, 'The LORD was with Joseph so that he prospered' (Gen. 39:2).

Here's the part of his story I know I would have found most hard to stomach. Not only had his brothers already rejected him, but when his master's wife tried to get him to sleep with her and he refused, she made up a story and he ended up in prison. Of course, his master sided with his wife, but what a reward for being upright! Joseph could have wallowed in self-pity, blamed God for all that had happened to him – and yet he didn't. We go on to read how God continued to be with him: 'While Joseph was there in the prison, the LORD was with him; he showed him kindness and granted him favour in the eyes of the prison warder' (Gen. 39:20–21).

Even in the midst of huge human rejection, God never left Joseph's side, and we read of the Lord's favour on him no matter how that rejection changed his physical circumstances. Ultimately, God turned around and used all that had happened to Joseph for his purposes. Joseph was still in prison at the time the Pharaoh was having troubling dreams. One of Pharaoh's servants had been imprisoned for a short time alongside Joseph and had experienced how he could interpret dreams. He suggested Pharaoh ask Joseph for his help. God revealed to Joseph the interpretations of Pharaoh's dreams and, in doing so, paved the way for Joseph to be elevated in status and position. He was then in just the right place to use his godly wisdom to help plan for the coming famine – as well as accept, forgive and help his brothers in their time of need.

Joseph's story speaks to me of how God is always near. It is interesting, however, to be reminded that he may not rescue us from the consequences of bad treatment from others, even if we think he should. What we can be sure of is that he will certainly never leave us, or forsake us.

Jesus: the proof God never rejects us

Of course, the proof of God's love is found in the cross. We have seen how Jesus was let down by his friends – they abandoned him right in his hour of need – so he can empathize with us when we feel let down and rejected by others. He was also despised by those who didn't like his message, and is described in Isaiah as one who epitomizes rejection: 'He was despised and rejected by mankind, a man of suffering, and familiar with pain. Like one from whom people hide their faces he was despised, and we held him in low esteem' (Isa. 53:3). If you ever feel like he can't understand the pain of rejection that you are going through, take some time to reflect on this verse. You *can* open your heart to him, because he *does* understand.

But there is something even more important to remember: on the cross, Jesus, quoting the opening line of Psalm 22, uttered the words: '"*Eloi, Eloi, lema sabachthani?*" (which means "My God, my God, why have you forsaken me?")' (Mark 15:34). This is so significant because it reveals to us that, even though he stayed in the will of the Father, he felt rejected by his father for a time. Why? Because it was the only way to ensure that *we* never have to be rejected by God. *That* is the value that God places on us. God could not look upon his sin-covered Son (see Hab. 1:13; 2 Cor. 5:21), and yet he allowed Jesus to suffer in our place. This means we can *always* be connected to, accepted and loved by God. When we truly allow that truth to sink into our hearts, the sense of security it blossoms within us can help us to see the fear and/or pain of rejection from a different perspective.

Dealing with rejection in everyday life

I know that I am mainly focusing on why we wear masks in church in this book, but our daily experiences continually feed our sense of identity and so I wanted to comment on rejection that is experienced elsewhere too. As a freelance writer, I experience the joys of having work accepted for publication – as well as the deep lows of other work being rejected. Even the journey I had with this book to get it to publication taught me a lot about how I deal with rejection in my professional life. I went through so many highs and lows, over a period of two and a half years, before finally signing a contract to publish what you are reading now. I had a huge amount of positive feedback, but ultimately many publishers chose not to publish my book. Even now, whenever publishers tell me that they don't feel my work is quite right for their publication or book list, if I'm honest, my pride does get hurt – and my sense of self is rocked a little.

I have to remind myself that, sometimes, it is not because my work is sub-standard but it simply does not fit into what they are currently looking for. At other times, I may need to work harder on a piece of writing. I have to be humble enough to recognize that. Sometimes, though, I need to simply remind myself that, while my ego has been bruised a little, my worth is not based on whether my writing is published somewhere or not. While I may have to allow myself a little bit of time for my emotional hurt to settle down, I can still rest in the knowledge that God *always* chooses me. *That* is what my life is based on; what my sense of worth and purpose should be built on too. Meditating on such truth is definitely healing balm for those tough times of rejection!

Openness and encouragement

I have learned over the years that so often our fears (and sins) have less power over us when we talk about them openly. The Bible teaches us to confess to one another: 'Therefore confess your sins to each other and pray for each other so that you may be healed' (Jas 5:16). So, one of the ways we can combat the fear of rejection is by admitting it to a close friend. That way they can speak truth to us, stand with us and support us. They can also speak words of encouragement over us – something else that the passage in Hebrews 10 exhorts us to do: 'Let us consider how we may spur one another on towards love and good deeds, not giving up meeting together, as some are in the habit of doing, but encouraging one another – and all the more as you see the Day approaching' (vv.24–25).

Learning to be truly open with someone close to us places us in a position to be able to receive encouragement from them – as well as give it ourselves. I love this statement, which I discovered when I was preparing a talk on encouragement, as it really speaks about how being part of a community and giving encouragement helps us too: 'When we speak words of encouragement to each other, we step out of the lonely world that we are in ourselves – by ourselves – and we enter in to the richer world of community – of the *other* – where we find ourselves more truly ourselves.'[5]

I know there is always a risk involved with any human relationship, and it can be particularly difficult to be open with others if we have experienced a lot of criticism in the past. However, we need to remember that there is such a wealth of richness to be

> Underneath the top, 'presentable' veneer most of us put on, each of us is struggling with something.

discovered when we do find friendships in which we can truly be ourselves, and so it is worth stepping out to discover them (see Chapter 16). Because underneath the top, 'presentable' veneer most of us put on, each of us is struggling with something. Each one of us needs that non-judgemental word of encouragement that reminds us that we are all works in progress. That God's grace and acceptance is for us today – not just for when we are all cleaned up and perfect.

Personal reflection

- Have you ever thought, 'If people really knew me they wouldn't love me'? How do you feel about the truth that people cannot truly love you without knowing the real you?
- What do you think your sense of worth and purpose is currently being built on?
- Take some time to soak in the truth that God *never* rejects you. Look over the scriptures that reinforce that message within this chapter (and find some more for yourself).

NB If rejection has been a really painful part of your life, don't move on quickly from this chapter, but take time to express yourself before God. Also, give space for the Holy Spirit to bring healing, comfort and peace into your heart (you may find the 'processing well' section found in Chapter 11 helpful to work through too).

Shame and Guilt

After moving back home to my husband, walking into our church was a *huge* step for me. While I may have dealt with the guilt over what I had done, I still had to face hurt friends – many for the first time. The feeling of shame as I walked over the threshold was immense – and one that I know the devil wanted to keep me locked into as he kept bringing it up. I had to learn to refuse to accept it. Allowing myself to be reached by others, as we worked through the process of forgiveness and rebuilding trust, was a big way of releasing myself from the power of shame.

Unfortunately, the twins 'shame' and 'guilt' can be rife within our church communities. To clarify the difference: guilt is the feeling we get when we have done something wrong (an action), whereas shame relates much more closely to who we are (sense of self). This means that guilt can trigger shame – yes we may have done something wrong, as I had, but we end up feeling that the problem is inherently within us; a part of us.

Sometimes past behaviour makes us closed. We don't want to open up our lives and share them closely with others in case people find out things about us that we are ashamed of. There are various reasons for this. Sadly, we may have experienced judgemental attitudes from others before. We could mistakenly

Taking Off the Mask

believe that someone's opinion of us matters more than God's (which we have seen is something that many of us can struggle with). Or we may wrongly believe that their opinion will reflect God's opinion, which isn't always going to be true.

When I think about shame, I am always drawn back to Mary – and Joseph. They begin the story of Jesus coming to earth as a man, and yet for that to happen they had to be willing to suffer the shame of her being pregnant while unwed. Their shame was not a result of their own actions, but the way they humbly faced it is inspiring. It teaches us the importance of not allowing shame to be a barrier between us and God. Both of them counted up the cost and were willing to be used by God no matter what people would say as a result.

Mary was a young woman but she was full of humble faith. I find it outstanding that, once the angel had revealed that she would be with child through the Holy Spirit even though she was still a virgin (see Luke 1), she simply said, 'I am the Lord's servant . . . May your word to me be fulfilled' (v.38). She must have known she risked rejection by her betrothed, Joseph, as well as by her family and neighbours. And what about the story she told people about having been given her child by the Holy Spirit? She must have realized that many would think that she had lost her mind. And yet she quietly submitted to God's will.

Joseph, too, was an unlikely candidate (in our eyes) for bringing up the infant Jesus. A lowly carpenter, he didn't have much going for him – apart from those heart qualities that God saw and loved. Even when he was struggling with what he thought was Mary's betrayal, we are told in Matthew 1:19 that he planned to divorce her quietly. And when an angel appeared to him to explain what was happening, again Joseph quietly and humbly accepted the truth, showing great faith and obedience.

When I think of how these two characters were willing to be seemingly disgraced by their own community when they were carrying out God's purposes, it makes me ponder those times when I've cared too much about what others think – or been too caught up in my own shame and guilt to see past them to God.

Redeeming our past

In recent years, due to the love and healing I have received from God, I have found myself being far more open about the more shameful aspects of my past than I ever thought possible. It isn't as if my opening line to newcomers in church is, 'I struggled with a victim mentality and it almost killed my marriage.' However, it is now much easier for me to open up and talk about my own experiences when I sense it is helpful for a person struggling with similar issues.

Sometimes when you have walked through a really difficult season, and done your fair share of sinning and rebelling, God brings you to a place of repentance. He then graciously shows you how he is able to redeem that part of your past (as we saw Jesus do with Peter in John 21). I believe that is an amazing gift from him. Steve and I decided to celebrate this gift when our first child was born. We had chosen her first name already, but wanted her middle name to reflect the fact that we were only still standing together because of his Grace. I love the reminder it is to me each time I see her full name written out.

When God redeems our mistakes, it doesn't mean the conse-quences magically disappear, but he gives us the strength and purpose to move through them without crumbling. We can see this clearly in the story of David. We know him, of course, as the shepherd who slew Philistine giant Goliath, and the king who God called 'a man after [my] own heart' (1 Sam. 13:14). And yet David messed up. Big time.[1]

His is a story that again fills me with encouragement. He seemed to have it all – the kingdom, a people who all followed him gladly and a great relationship with God. But then he allowed his gaze to rest for too long on Bathsheba . . . He quickly began to justify all sorts of ever more sinful behaviour in his mind: taking her for himself, trying to get her husband to sleep with her to cover his tracks and eventually having her husband killed on the battlefield (see 2 Sam. 11).

I can easily imagine what was going through David's mind as he descended that slippery slope, as so much of it resonates with my own self-justifications over the years. But here's the thing: when Nathan the prophet confronted David's sin in 2 Samuel 12, David suddenly realized what he had been doing and immediately repented: 'I have sinned against the Lord.' It seems like another 'unmasking' moment and David graduated from it well, repenting deeply and sincerely.

David and Bathsheba still had to deal with the difficult consequences of their actions – losing their son. But David's repentance and honesty before God (take a look at the whole of Psalm 51, which was written at this time) meant that he was not cut off from him. Here are a few of the verses:

> Create in me a pure heart, O God,
>> and renew a steadfast spirit within me.
> Do not cast me from your presence
>> or take your Holy Spirit from me.
> Restore to me the joy of your salvation
>> and grant me a willing spirit, to sustain me (vv.10–12).

He could have spiralled into a pit of shame but David faced up to his sin, turned from it and restored his relationship with his heavenly Father. As the above verses show, the relationship was such an important part of his life, and, once his mask was removed, he was able to see how it had been affected. His approach is a model we can follow today too, instead of allowing our shame to become the mask we hide behind.

Letting shame rob us

Carrie Lloyd, who writes a blog about navigating the world of Christian dating, wrote a book called *The Virgin Monologues*, which I had the pleasure of editing.[2] She was very honest within it, including her struggles with shame over having had sexual relationships in her twenties as well as a porn addiction. Having been out of the church for a while, coming back into it she found that being around well-meaning twenty-somethings, whose goals included marrying a virgin, compounded her feelings of shame and guilt. Her journey of learning not to listen to the shame whispering in her ear, which was robbing her of her sense of self-worth and all hope of a future, really resonated with me. I asked her to comment on why she thinks shame so often plagues people within churches:

> I'm of the belief that shame is not a God-made emotion, but an evil distortion of guilt. Guilt is found in the making of a mistake – otherwise known as conviction. 'Guilt says I've made a mistake', as Brené Brown put it in a recent TED Talk, while 'Shame says I am a mistake'.
> The conviction I have is a cause of celebration – not because I made a mistake but because I'm close enough to know God's heart

for my life. It means I can hear his voice, as opposed to rejecting all guilt in fear of carrying too much shame. It is vital to keep a close conversation in all endeavours with the Lord, but carrying shame around can only lead us to dead ends. The victim mentality is when everything is our fault, and we can never get anything right. Or it's everyone else's fault, because the shame is too much to bear. We become defeatist. Hopeless.

Overcoming our wrongs has to take more strength, more personal relationship with the Lord and with conviction comes a turning around, comes a growth pattern, comes a change. Shame does nothing but melt away any hope we might have had for change. Why else did the enemy distort guilt in the first place? To separate you from the Lord, to dilute your intimacy.

Within the comfort of the secret place, he disciplines me in a warming and hopeful way, with encouragement, pushing past the despair I may have created, and pushing through to a cure, to an amendment.

Two of the strongest areas that try to keep us in shame are pornography and sexual impurity. Shame creates such a fear of being rejected, we hide away, isolating ourselves from others and therefore reality. But shame doesn't bring life, only more secrecy, and it is only so long until we are grasping for breath, for freedom, for a break into the big wide world again.

> Shame creates such a fear of being rejected, we hide away, isolating ourselves from others and therefore reality.

One of the other ways shame can keep us locked up is when we take on the shame of a past that was not our fault at all. When someone else was abusive, and yet we feel weighed down by blame ourselves. Perhaps we were physically or verbally abused, or our parents were alcoholics.

Joy suffered abuse in childhood, and here describes what it feels like to take on guilt and shame as a result:

> Being emotionally and sexually abused as a child not only robs you of innocence, it also causes a heavy weight of guilt and shame to be wrongly assumed. Someone else is at fault but we bear the brunt of our unwilling participation, our inability to say no or to run away.
>
> For years this was my dark cloak and covering, largely invisible but ever-present, because I failed to fully appreciate my new clothing in Christ. Instead of wearing filthy rags of guilt and shame, believers in him are to consider themselves clothed in a garment of salvation, wrapped in a mantle of mercy and covered by a robe of righteousness, all imputed to us by his work on the cross.
>
> Even now, as a mature adult, I still struggle sometimes not to say sorry for everything or apologize for breathing, so acute is my sense of shame and wrongdoing. However, I am learning to better accept who I am in Christ, to rest in his love and to see myself as God sees me – not a victim but a victor, not a mistake but a marvellous creation, not a guilt-ridden girl but a grace-redeemed woman of faith.

True and false guilt

As Carrie noted earlier, true guilt is actually a result of a sin. The feeling comes as our conscience is pricked by the Holy Spirit in order for us to acknowledge it, repent and allow God's forgiveness to flow in. This restores our relationship with him. In this way, guilt can be extremely helpful. However, since the beginning of the world humans have had a tendency to hate that feeling of guilt, so we try to avoid it by suppressing it. We can also feel that opening up and confessing to God is too painful and, if we do, he will *have* to punish us severely and so we try to hide our guilt from him, which is a futile exercise. (Adam and Eve found that out when they tried to hide their nakedness from him.)

The truth is, throughout the Bible God is described as a forgiving God to those who confess to him (1 John 1:9 says that 'If we confess our sins, he is faithful and just and will forgive us our sins and purify us from all unrighteousness'). I really like the comment that Will van der Hart and Rob Waller make in *The Guilt Book*: 'The great twist in Genesis 3 is not only that God can see straight through any fig leaf, but that he actually makes a better covering for Adam and Eve in the form of some animal skins.'[3] To be able to benefit from the 'new clothing' that God will provide for us, we have to remove our masks. Hebrews encourages us to lay ourselves bare before God, so we can be cleansed by him: 'Let us draw near to God with a sincere heart and with the full assurance that faith brings, having our hearts sprinkled to cleanse us from a guilty conscience and having our bodies washed with pure water' (Heb. 10:22).

Admitting our guilt

It is so hard to admit to people when we have done something wrong, though, isn't it? Even now, I find it toe-curlingly difficult. And yet, the sad fact is that we don't realize how much of a burden it is, carrying guilt around. It's far heavier than the short-

> We don't realize how much of a burden it is, carrying guilt around.

lived embarrassment we might feel about being honest about our failings. We try to cover over the parts we don't like – even trying to hide them from God. We've just seen how God made

Adam and Eve new clothing, but before that they tried to cover the parts of themselves they were now embarrassed by. They were also, no doubt, weighed down by the guilt they felt due to disobeying God.

In order to be set free from that heavy sense of guilt, we do need to humble ourselves before God and admit our mistakes – as well as our need for his help. As I've already mentioned, I think our culture can heavily influence us and it certainly champions the independent, self-sufficient approach to life. But it is also part of our basic sinful nature: it hates to feel any sort of dependence towards anything other than itself. It can be hard to throw that off long enough to be truly humble. And yet it is a vital part of the process – as is remembering that God longs for us to admit our wrongdoings so that he can wash us clean of them and free us from the terrible feelings of guilt.

When church compounds our guilty feelings

Van der Hart and Waller comment in their book that anthropology suggests that false guilt has been used throughout history as a means of social control. This can, sadly, be seen within Christianity's history. It can also occur within individual churches in which leaders try to get members to do what they want by making them feel guilty until they do. The term 'heavy shepherding' was bandied around in the 1980s to describe such control-heavy 'discipleship'. As a child of about 9, I experienced this first hand as our seemingly loving pastor became more and more controlling, demanding that people ask permission before they did even the simplest of things. It wasn't long before a whole group of us left to find another church (see Chapter 11 for more on this).

We do not earn our salvation, so such approaches within church life fly in the face of what God intends for his people. He does call for obedience, but our motivation is love and gratitude for what he has already done for us. But when a church's congregation is led by someone motivating them through false guilt this distorts the truth. It also lays individuals open to their own personal struggle with false guilt.

The same can be true for a church that is prone to legalism, although the leadership may not be intending to manipulate in any way. But legalism can cause people to feel guilty about a whole host of different things. Jesus spoke out against legalism, openly criticizing religious leaders for it (see my previous comments on Matt. 23 in Chapter 8). Bizarrely, many churches have their own hidden list of dos and don'ts – and when this is married with a legalistic approach, people can be left wracked with guilt.

Whatever church we are in, there can be instances in which people are labelled using a hierarchy based on their 'past sins'. This isn't necessarily a conscious thing, but those people who were once drug addicts or sexually promiscuous, for example, can be left feeling less worthy, as Carrie mentioned, even though they have confessed before God and received his forgiveness. Our human-ness can unfortunately make us judgemental, and anyone who is struggling, or has struggled in the past, with any sort of sin can begin to feel like they aren't good enough for church.

It is desperately important for us all to realize that God loves us totally, unconditionally. The reality of the Christian message is that we are *all* undeserving of his love. None of us fares better than another

> Without Jesus, the verdict for us all is guilty. For those who are in Christ, the verdict is not guilty. End of story.

when the measuring stick of God's holiness is held up against us, because we all fall short of perfection. And yet God reaches out to us all, irrespective of who we are or what we have done. Without Jesus, the verdict for us all is guilty. For those who are in Christ, the verdict is not guilty. End of story.

Early origins of false guilt

It isn't just the church environment that can cause us to feel guilty. Sometimes our upbringing can reinforce those first feelings of guilt that we can get as we start learning more independence – and begin to understand whether an action is allowed or not during our toddler years. Negative parenting techniques constantly criticize whenever a child does even the smallest thing wrong, and the result can be that the child withdraws into itself, internalizing feelings of guilt and shame. Over the years, those feelings continue to be carried and adults can feel angry and guilty, defaulting into self-blame (see the section on our inner critical voices in Chapter 5 for more on this).

Pushing past guilt and shame

We have looked at how as humans we hate guilt and shame, and so we try to hide these feelings. We can also have a tendency to try to avoid situations in which we are prone to feel them. This can include leaving church before people have time to talk to us at the end of a service or even ensuring friendships remain at a shallow level so people don't have a chance to discover the parts of us we feel ashamed of. But, as mentioned before, the

Bible teaches us to confess our sins to one another (Jas. 5:16) and to bear one another's burdens (Gal. 6:1–2).

Some of us can use serving within church as a means of self-punishment, doing more in an effort to make ourselves feel better. This can remain hidden, because we can feel ashamed that we haven't been able to fully grasp hold of God's message of grace. Acknowledging all of this and opening up to someone we trust can be the first step to stopping this destructive cycle.

Having someone to walk alongside us, who can gently point out to us if we start to take on unnecessary guilt again, can be so valuable in our journey away from guilt and shame. Being able to admit our difficulties to someone we trust, who will encourage us to confess our sins in order for healing and freedom to come, is so helpful.

Letting go

Ultimately, Jesus reminds us to come to him: 'Come to me, all you who are weary and burdened, and I will give you rest. Take my yoke upon you and learn from me, for I am gentle and humble in heart, and you will find rest for your souls. For my yoke is easy and my burden is light' (Matt. 11:28–30). We cannot take up his yoke without laying down our own first.

A yoke is a wooden harness that links together a pair of animals, usually oxen, which helps them pull a load together. Our guilt, or shame, can be things that weigh us down heavily, and stop us from making progress. The first step is actually acknowledging that we do not need to carry that burden around any longer; that we do not need, in fact, to do anything to be acceptable to him. He longs to teach us how to work in tandem with him – using his yoke, which is full of forgiveness, grace and power and is so much easier than the alternative.

I understand that it can sometimes seem like the secrets that we have kept inside for so long, out of a sense of shame, are far too big to let go. But the cross is enough even for those things that we would hate for our church friends to know about! I saw how beautifully God worked in a friend's life on this very issue when I sent a few of this book's chapters to her in preparation for a speaking event. As she read the chapters, God began to speak to her about an issue of shame from her past that she had never quite pieced together before – and had certainly never spoken to anyone about. I am so humbled by how God used my writing, but that is not why I'm including this anecdote. She later testified that it was as she opened up and told me about the shame that she realized she was giving it over to God – and he took it from her once and for all. She now feels lighter and knows that that shame has lost its power over her.[4]

Visualization exercise

If you know that shame is something that you struggle with, perhaps the following may help you, as I found it incredibly powerful when I came across the suggestion.[5]

Read through the following Scripture, to remind yourself of the power of the cross:

> When you were dead in your sins and in the uncircumcision of your flesh, God made you alive with Christ. He forgave us all our sins, having cancelled the charge of our legal indebtedness, which stood against us and condemned us; he has taken it away, nailing it to the cross (Col. 2:13–14).

Prayerfully consider what it is that you know shames you, and still has a hold on you. Write it down and then close your eyes and visualize taking and pinning that paper to the cross. Stay with the image until you see God take the paper and crumple it. Once you have done that, you may wish to crumple the physical paper you have, before throwing it away. Take some time to pray, asking God to replace that shame with his love and peace. You may find it helpful to tell a friend about what you have done (either beforehand or afterwards).

Personal reflection

- Can you recognize in yourself a tendency to hide from your sins rather than admit them? We do not need to be ashamed of our guilt – it is the Holy Spirit nudging us to get ourselves right with God again. Could you take some time to bring before God any guilt that he places on your heart now?
- Have you ever been influenced by someone who made you feel guilty until you did what they wanted you to? Do you now recognize that was a false guilt? Ask God to take away any lingering sense of guilt or shame.
- Do you struggle with a sense of shame? Is there anyone you can talk this through with and ask them to support you? You may also find it helpful to take some time to work through the visualization exercise, if you haven't already done so.

Disappointment

This is one of the reasons for mask-wearing that upsets me most, because it so often means that someone has been let down by their church in the past. They wear a mask because they've tried being honest and open before and were really hurt by the response they received. Perhaps people judged them or simply didn't know how to deal with what they were being told so turned away rather than coming alongside and accepting the other person regardless of their story.

In the responses I had to my survey, there were some who said they had been part of a church that had an abusive culture. They walked away from going to any church for a time, as they felt it had disappointed them so much that it robbed them of their faith. How awful – and sad. There are no words for such tragedy. As mentioned previously, as a child I lived through an experience that I didn't fully understand at the time. We were part of a lively, evangelical church and I loved going there. But gradually, month by month, I noticed people were more on edge – the pastor was more 'in control'. Here is how my mum described that time to me:

Having started a Bible-based, very family-oriented church that grew very fast, had excellent teaching, and was a happy place where many strong friendships started, the pastor seemed to totally change direction. From being a man who, for about two years, delegated leaders in the areas of children's work, worship, preaching and so on, he sent us all a letter saying that nothing at all was allowed to be said or done without his foreknowledge and approval. There was no more freedom in our times of worship and people became miserable and unhappy. Many left to seek other churches and a few he had sent abroad as missionaries were totally abandoned, left with no means of support at all.

That pastor was certainly abusing his position, and those who had joined the church in good faith were increasingly alarmed and disappointed by his behaviour. When he refused to see he was doing anything wrong, a whole group of people, including my family, left the church.

There are so many people walking around with a huge amount of pain and hurt because of the disappointments they have experienced in church. The sad thing is, it can cause people to turn away from church – and sometimes even from God too, as the pain and hurt inflicted by others is somehow merged with their picture of who God is.

Mistreated and cast out

When I think about disappointment I often think about Hagar, and wonder how she must have felt alone in the desert with her son, having been sent away by Abram (later renamed Abraham).

As she spent time in their community, Hagar must have come to understand more about the God that Abram and his family worshipped. They were, after all, following what God had asked them to do by specifically living a nomadic lifestyle (see Gen. 12:1–3). She would have heard about the special covenant God had made with Abram. I don't know what her expectations would have been as part of Abram's household, but I suspect she may well have believed she would be better treated because of their deep faith.

Hagar may also have been quite close to Sarai (later renamed Sarah), as it was Sarai who suggested Abram sleep with Hagar to get the heir God had promised them (see Gen. 16:1–4). While it may seem strange to us, this was a custom allowed in those times back in Ur, where they came from: if a wife could not conceive, she gave a servant to her husband and any resulting children were seen as the wife's. We are not told how Hagar felt about this arrangement, but it could have meant a change in her position – for the better – as she would have been seen as a concubine or second wife (see v.3). When I read the story, through my modern eyes, it does seem thoughtless that they simply assumed Hagar would be a surrogate. Although Hagar did seem to take advantage of the situation to lord it over her mistress at times . . .

It was at the point that Hagar became pregnant that things began to unravel. As soon as Abram and Sarai took the matter into their own hands, rather than trusting in God, disappointment, jealousy, anger and pain became a part of the story.

Abram's supposedly faith-filled household was being torn apart due to their own actions (which revealed their lack of faith). However, even after Hagar ran away because she had wound up her mistress and Sarai had in turn mistreated her, it appeared that God was redeeming the situation. An angel of the Lord appeared to Hagar and told her to go back and submit to her mistress. This 'angel of the Lord' seems to have been God himself, and is the first instance recorded in the Bible of God appearing to someone after the fall. It is also the first time he named a child that was still in the womb. Isn't that amazing? God was reaching out to the one who had felt so let down she ran away.[1] He spoke to the one who was used to being treated as a slave. He began by asking her questions that allowed her to speak freely.

As a result of God's visit, Hagar called him 'the One who sees me' (see Gen. 16:7–16). It seems like, for the first time in this story, she felt she was known and loved. Isn't that what we are all longing for? That was enough for her to humble herself, repent and go back into a situation that she had been deeply disappointed by previously – and without any indication that Sarai would treat her any better than before. They did live peacefully for a time, but sadly – not that long after Sarai had had her son – Abraham (as he was now called) sent Hagar and Ishmael into the wilderness, because having them around upset his wife.

Thrust out into the desert, Hagar *must* have questioned why she had ever trusted and grown close to Abraham and Sarah – and indeed God himself. She may have felt bitter, mistreated, put upon – all manner of negative emotions could have been swallowing her up. In Genesis 21 we see her in absolute despair: she has run out of water and has put her son just out of her eye line as she can't bear to watch him die (see vv.14–16). If anyone had a reason to be crushed by disappointment, it was Hagar. *But* ...

The rest of the chapter describes how God heard her crying, supplied their need for water and, indeed, looked after them as the boy grew into a man (vv.17–21). It wasn't the life that Hagar had imagined – for herself or her child. Having borne the heir to Abraham's family she must have assumed that she would be honoured – and certainly looked after and kept safe. But God was there with them even when they ended up in that desert place.

Sometimes the same happens to us. We may be let down and/or hurt by others in the church, but we can often blame God when he is actually the only constant in the situation. He hasn't changed and, however others may treat us, God will never let us down. That doesn't mean he protects us from how other people may treat us – and that is something many of us can find difficult, especially when their behaviour is totally unacceptable.

> We may be hurt by others in the church, but we can often blame God when he is actually the only constant in the situation.

Church = people = mistakes

Sometimes we can approach church with unrealistic expectations of what it will provide for us. Interestingly, Carl Jung said that institutions can become like artificial mothers to us; when we look to them for love we are disappointed, and then we also experience the guilt of being a disappointment.[2] We need to remember that church is full of people. We are all human, we will all make mistakes and let one another down – but that isn't a reason to stop the journey of deepening friendships (although we may need to challenge one another on our behaviour at times). It didn't stop Jesus from gathering what was quite a motley bunch of disciples around him to 'do life' with them, and I do believe he can teach us how to cultivate the same sort of deep friendships (see Chapter 16). Just like a family bears with one another, so we are called to love and care for one another (John 13:34–35, Rom. 12:10, Gal. 6:2).[3]

There can be times when we expect too much from another person. When we let them see the real 'us', but then want them to come up with all the answers for the issues we are finding difficult and confusing. We need to be honest about our expectations of others too. And, actually, it isn't always helpful for people to give us answers. Sometimes it is simply the act of a friend coming alongside us and being willing to journey with us, whatever we are going through, that helps us to move forward and find the answers for ourselves.

I do realize that there are times when the wisest thing to do is step away from a friendship that has become more toxic than life-giving. This can be gut-wrenchingly difficult to do, and can also have an effect on our very being by shaking our sense of identity. Just as I began working through this chapter again, the wonderful author and speaker Jennifer Rees Larcombe posted on her ministry Facebook page a picture of a ladybird her friend had taken just after it had emerged from its pupa state.[4] She said it took seven hours before the red and black spots appeared – the picture showed it to be yellow-orangeish in colour. Jennifer likened that ladybird to how we can feel when we have lost something – such as a damaging relationship – colourless and drained. And yet she reminded us how the ladybird had to wait for her permanent colours to appear – and that God often does that when he transforms us through such difficulties and disappointments. What a beautiful, and timely, picture.

Disappointed with Jesus?

We will all face disappointments, big and small, throughout our lives. And yes, some of those disappointments will be tied up with God's people. But let's remember that even those who lived alongside Jesus were disappointed at times. His followers were often confused by what he said and did, because his ideas of what kingdom living meant were so totally different to theirs. The people of Israel had longed for, and expected, a mighty saviour who would sweep in and save them from the oppressive Roman regime. But Jesus talked about turning the other cheek and said that he 'did not come to be served, but to serve, and to give his life as a ransom for many' (Matt. 20:28). It must have seemed so strange and topsy-turvy to them – in fact, some of his disciples did leave after hearing his teaching (see John 6:60–69).

Jesus was calling his disciples to a life in which they gave up control and their own expectations – and became vulnerable. When he left them hanging, without clear explanation (see Acts 1:7, where he says, 'It is not for you to know'), he must have known the disappointment his disciples would have felt. And yet, I have a sense that the purpose behind that disappointment was, as Mark Yaconelli suggests, to see God, themselves and others more honestly.[5]

There are other, extremely perplexing, episodes within Jesus' encounters with his friends. I do wonder how Lazarus' sisters Mary and Martha must have felt when their brother died. They considered Jesus a good friend, and had seen him teach and do miracles, and yet where was he when Lazarus died? Beforehand, they had sent word to Jesus that their brother was ill, saying 'Lord the one you love is ill' (John 11:3), presumably expecting him to hurry back. But what did Jesus do? He stayed where he was for two more days (vv.6–7). It is important to notice the connecting word at the start of verse 6: 'So'. We are being told that *because* Jesus heard the news about Lazarus he decided to stay where he was a little longer. He knew what he was going to do, and that raising Lazarus from the dead would glorify God more than healing him before his death. The family didn't have this knowledge though . . .

By the time Jesus' group arrived, Lazarus had been dead for four days (v.17). We are told that Martha went out to meet him straight away, but Mary did not. In both their minds, they must have been wondering why Jesus had taken so long. His appearance may have allowed hope to rise in their hearts, and then they would have had to stifle it again because their brother was already dead. They both said to Jesus that if he had been there earlier Lazarus would not have died. Their grief and disappointment in Jesus must have been huge. And yet, even then, Jesus did not immediately go to their brother's tomb but wept alongside Mary. We are taught that this reveals his humanity and depth of love for the family, but how that must have confused them!

Eventually Jesus called Lazarus out of the tomb, raising him from the dead. The delay in reaching Lazarus gave Jesus an opportunity to show he has power over death itself. But for the sisters, it must have been so hard to deal with Jesus not turning up when they felt they needed him most.

I am sure some of our own disappointments are based in our assumptions about how situations and circumstances should be. God has perfect timing – even if we are impatient or hurt by a seeming delay. He often does things in ways we don't understand or don't like. While he sees the overall picture, we get hurt and disappointed that the part right in front of us isn't as we expected it to be. Often it seems to go against what we've been taught to believe about God, but we need to gently remind ourselves that we can't put him in a box! He may use the things we go through to try to show us a different perspective – and to open us up to a deeper experience of his love and acceptance.

Sarah Walton suffers from Lyme disease; she knows exactly what it feels like for life to turn out differently to her expectations. Through painful difficulties, she has come to understand that: 'Circumstances that perplex us need not drive us to despair. Instead, they can take us to new depths of faith. They challenge us to trust solely in the promises of God, rather than creating a god of our own design in order to make sense of what perplexes us.'[6]

We don't understand when God allows difficulties, but he knows how they will display his glory eventually (see John 9:3 – that's a hard one to understand!). He also often steps in to circumstances where others have mistreated us and redeems those for his purposes.

Perhaps we have to ask ourselves whether we truly believe God can redeem *any* situation. Towards the end of her encounter with Jesus, and while her brother was still in his tomb, Martha's faith levels rose again and she was able to declare with confidence her trust in who Jesus is: 'I believe that you are the Messiah, the Son of God, who is to come into the world' (John 11:27). Please do notice that she said that *before* Lazarus was raised. It reminds me of the moment in the book of Daniel where Shadrach, Meshach and Abednego were about to be thrown into the fiery furnace for refusing to bow down and worship the golden image that King Nebuchadnezzar of Babylon had had erected. As they faced what looked like certain death, they confidently said, 'If we are thrown into the blazing furnace, the God we serve is able to deliver us from it, and he will deliver us from Your Majesty's hand. But even if he does not, we want you to know, Your Majesty, that we will not serve your gods or worship the image of gold you have set up' (Dan. 3:17–18).

Martha, Shadrach, Meshach and Abednego all clung to what they knew about God. Understanding more about his character helps us to be sustained even when we don't understand his ways; even through severe disappointment.

Allowing disappointment to draw us towards God

It seems that one of the things biblical characters can teach us about disappointment is how it can draw us *towards* God, not away from him. Just think about how disappointed David must have been when he was on the run from his own son Absalom! By that point in his life he'd had a successful reign, and been loved by the people, but his own son had turned on him and seized power. So much of what happened, we learn from Nathan's prophecy, was due to David's own sin (see 2 Sam. 12:11–12), and yet he didn't dwell on the deception or his own failings – rather he turned to God and declared how he trusted him. Scholars believe that the beautiful Psalm 23 was penned during this time, as was Psalm 3, in which he stated, 'Lord, how many are my foes! How many rise up against me!' (v.1). However, he declared that God was his shield and went on to say that:

> I lie down and sleep;
>> I wake again, because the LORD sustains me.
> I will not fear though tens of thousands
>> assail me on every side (vv.5–6).

How amazing to be able to say that, even though he faced opposition and treachery from within his own family. He must have reached a point of being able to forgive those who had wronged him (we see that in how he handled himself before Saul, even when Saul was trying to kill him!). It can be so hard to even contemplate the idea of forgiveness when someone has hurt and disappointed us deeply. However, if we believe in the forgiveness of God, and enjoy it for ourselves when we repent of any wrongdoing, we need to accept that God forgives those who have hurt us too – if they repent before him.

When I was really struggling with the way the other person involved in my leaving my husband had hurt me, I picked up a copy of R.T. Kendall's *Total Forgiveness*. It was a life-changing experience for me. I had been wrestling with bitterness and unforgiveness, and then feeling guilty about that because my husband had so wonderfully extended his forgiveness towards me! I seemed trapped in a self-destructive cycle, with emotions that were eating me up inside. But R.T.'s words explained to me clearly for the first time how withholding forgiveness actually causes us a great deal of harm, whereas it doesn't affect the other person who hurt us at all! I had a sudden realization that in order to care for and love myself, and also be the wife my husband deserved, I needed to forgive. I have shared that difficult lesson with many others in the years since and seen it release so much freedom.

We don't need to concern ourselves whether the other person has repented or not (sometimes we won't know) – that is between them and God, as we are not called to be their judge (see Jas 4:12). Extending our forgiveness towards them is about setting ourselves free, as only God is able to forgive and release them from their sin.

I know that walking the path of forgiveness is excruciatingly difficult, but we *can* keep laying this issue at the foot of the cross any time we seem to be dwelling on it again. I know that, while devastating for my life at the time, what I went through was not as horrific as some of the things that you may have experienced.

So let me simply add in a quote from Jill Drake, who was a victim of rape in her own home: 'I believe forgiveness gives you freedom. Freedom to move on without being held back by the past.' Her rape was known as the 'Ealing Vicarage Rape' and the shocking sentencing and media coverage caused a public outcry on the way rape victims were treated. This led to a change in the law – and Jill continued to fight for victims' rights throughout her life.[7]

Breaking free from disappointment

The most helpful teaching I have ever heard on the subject of disappointment was by Wendy Mann, a leader at the King's Arms Church in Bedford. She has visited many churches around the world as a speaker, and believes that hidden disappointment is slowly killing the church. I heard her speak at a local women's event, where she told us that so many of us are trying to live out our Christian lives desperate to show we are full of faith, and

> Hidden disappointment is slowly killing the church.

yet our efforts are being suffocated. This is because we are living with disappointment that we haven't worked through, and may not have admitted to anyone else – or even ourselves. Rather than expecting God to be good all the time, often we are expecting disappointment. We feel we cannot hope for too much from him, or his people, because we don't want to be disappointed again. And we don't want to encourage others to expect too much, as we don't want them to feel the pain either.

Sometimes this almost subconscious response is because we have not processed past events that caused us disappointment.

We can find phrases about God's goodness – either in the Bible or spoken by those around us – difficult to accept. The truth can't reach our hearts because it reaches as far as the disappointment and then gets stuck.

When I first heard Wendy speak everything inside of me was shouting 'Yes! Yes! Yes! This is what we need to preach about more – and learn how to do.' If we want to be free of disappointment then we need to process it well. We are lying to ourselves when we simply squash down the hurt and say we are walking in faith instead! We are also hurting others when we instruct them to simply tell any feelings of disappointment that they have no place, without giving them the space to work through why they have the feelings in the first place. We need to be real. We can't simply skip over this difficult, messy part in order to get to the positive outcome.

We *do* need to be thankful for what we have seen God do, even in difficult circumstances, but we also need to process any disappointment. We need to give other people permission and space to work through their own disappointment too. But do churches do that on a regular basis? Too often we want to make things better, fast, so we don't allow the space needed for this. It is as if we want to brush this process under the carpet because it isn't good for our PR (see Chapter 12), but God never does. The Bible is full of disappointed people who bring their confusion to God in the form of lament (the psalms are full of them, for example).

Processing well

Here are some practical ways we can give ourselves space and time to work through disappointment. I hope you find them as helpful as I have. While this may seem like an easy 'how to' list, they are just pointers and general principles. Each one of us has an individual journey with God that isn't 'one-size-fits-all'. You may need to take more time to work through the process, perhaps with a trusted friend or counsellor. However long it takes, the important thing is to acknowledge your disappointment and start working through it:[8]

• Begin by simply talking to God. Be brutally honest with him – don't worry if there are tears, shouting and the like, as the process can be messy. You are not dishonouring him by speaking truthfully, as he knows how you feel anyway. He simply longs to connect with you on a deeper level through you opening up to him.

   I find it so freeing when I do this – my journal is full of anguished words written when I have been in the throes of expressing my deepest disappointments and questions to God. I have learned that God does not mind me asking 'Why?' or crying out 'How long Lord?' In fact, doing so draws me closer to him because I am turning to him in my despair. (The Bible tells us that he is close to those who are hurting and comforts those who mourn – see Ps. 34:18 and Matt. 5:4.) I may not always get the answers I seek, however, and I have learned to accept that that is up to God (see Isa. 55:8), but he meets me in the midst of my questions.

   So tell him how you feel about your disappointment – you can vent as much as you like, as he will not belittle how you are feeling but will continue to love you as you express yourself. Do take care not to accuse him though. Being careful with your language will help with this – if you say, 'You abandoned me,' you are accusing him of abandoning you. But if you say, 'It felt like you abandoned me,' you are simply describing the feeling rather than asserting it as truth.

If we realize we have taken offence with God, we need to acknowledge that this is wrong thinking because, while it may *feel* like God doesn't love us when he allows us to go through difficulties, that simply isn't the truth. It can be helpful to remind ourselves that God's character, including his goodness towards us, doesn't change. It is our circumstances that we are disappointed with, or the fact that he hasn't done things the way we wanted or expected him to.

- Turn to the Psalms and read through them until you find one that expresses the emotions that you are experiencing in your disappointment. Stay there, engaging with it. Allow yourself to feel that pain, to let it come to the surface and connect with it.

  I recently read how Esther Fleece, when finally confronted with all the painful hurt and disappointment from her past that she had spent so long ignoring and covering over, discovered a psalm that echoed *exactly* the lament that had just bubbled out of her towards God. Each line seemed to follow one of the precise phrases she had just said herself.[9]

- Having found a psalm that has engaged you where you are at, now begin to do what so many of the psalmists did: turn your focus towards God, reminding yourself of the truth about his character and your standing before him as his child. This is what happens in a number of the psalms – take a look at Psalm 42 to see how David shares how desperate he is for a touch from God. His soul is panting for God, tears have been his constant companion and others have taunted him asking where his God is. He seems to be in utter despair, and yet he keeps reminding himself to put his trust in God, speaking directly to his soul. He determines to remember God and remind himself of how God's love is always present.

In her book, *No More Faking Fine*, Esther Fleece describes how she felt that seeing the psalmist remember God's goodness gave her the courage to believe that she could do the same. Remembering became a source of healing for her, and she talks about how God taught her a new way to grieve, through an intimate and honest conversation with him.

- Be gentle with yourself if you find you keep trying to analyse what is going on. Our brains can often work against us in this process. Remind yourself that Proverbs 3:5 talks about not leaning on your own understanding. We can often say to ourselves, 'If only I could understand what is going on I could have peace.' However, the truth is that the peace of God 'transcends all understanding' (Phil. 4:7).

The key to receiving peace from God is laying down our right to understand what is going on. That can be so hard when we are going through difficult times, but by surrendering our rights we are acknowledging God's sovereignty. Jesus did the same at the Garden of Gethsemane when he openly poured out his anguished heart to God, but ultimately submitted to him: 'Yet not as I will, but as you will' (Matt. 26:39).

- It may be that you know you have only managed to touch the surface of the disappointment you have felt over the years as you do this. Don't despair about that; sometimes God allows us *not* to feel things when they are too traumatic for us. He may be taking us on a journey so that we can work through them bit by bit, as we are able to cope with the emotions. He is ever gracious, patient and tender.

I know that living with the uncertainty and disappointment of unanswered prayer can be really difficult. It can cause me to shut down, become cynical or fearful. As a pastor's wife, there have been times in church meetings when I felt that I 'ought' to be praying for people to be healed, and yet I simply couldn't. Everything in me felt like a hypocrite, as most people in our congregation know that my mum is incredibly ill, suffering from fourteen different conditions that cause immense pain, and she is wheelchair-bound most of the time. The truth is, her healing is not down to me, but somehow I want to be able to explain why she hasn't been healed. But striving in my own strength gets me nowhere – apart from into an emotional muddle.

Healing is a mystery I know I will not fully understand until I get to heaven, and I have had to get to a place where I have let go of the right to know why some are healed while others aren't. I have learned to rejoice in the miracles we have seen, and believe it is vital to do so, but still have to work through disappointment at times – especially when I see up close how much Mum is suffering. I know it has affected my level of faith for seeing other people healed and, again, I have to consciously lay down my unbelief and choose to walk with God, partnering with him to outwork his purposes with those around me that he may be waiting to minister to through me.

It isn't easy, and there are days when I hear the pain and deep sadness in my mum's voice over the phone and I feel totally helpless. I have no words that can bring comfort – I can only acknowledge what is happening and reiterate that I love her. But then I often bring the jumble of emotions that I feel afterwards to God, wrestling with the anguish of confusion and hopelessness and crying out to him to relieve her pain. Sometimes I have to sit there in distress for a while, but I recognize that he is there with me in it. A sense of peace comes upon me and I know that, whether I understand what is going on or not, he loves my mum. I can trust him with her life, whether he heals her in this lifetime or not.

Personal reflection

- Have you ever felt a disappointment so deep in the way others have treated you that it has caused you to move away from God? Why do you think it had such an effect on your relationship with God?
- Take some time to think about the question that Mark Yaconelli posed: 'How might your disappointment invite you to see God, yourself and others more honestly?'
- If you know that you are struggling with disappointment right now, could you take some time to work through the 'processing well' section in this chapter, if you haven't already done so?

Church Culture

We live in a world of comparison, judgementalism and individualism. The effects are all around us – and they are encouraging us to pretend. The atmosphere in our churches is sometimes no different – and there can also be unspoken expectations that cause us to keep up a front rather than admit that we are struggling.

Sometimes it's our very theology that can make us feel like we have to hide our struggles. As Christians, we are told that we are new creations, but we can sometimes respond to that by feeling condemned. We have a sense of who we are called to be, but, if we are still acting in a certain way, still struggling with a particular addiction or other sin, we feel as though we've failed. We allow the enemy to heap feelings of guilt upon our heads, forgetting that there is 'now no condemnation for those who are in Christ Jesus' (Rom. 8:1).

The truth is that, 'In all these things we are more than conquerors through [Christ] who loved us' (Rom. 8:37). But somehow Christian sub-culture can, at times, emphasize such parts of the Bible while ignoring others. What about all the stories of people who, even though they knew God, messed up over and over again? The Bible is (thankfully!) full of such people (what

about Abraham, Sarah, Moses, Jonah and Peter to name a few?).
It is a huge, unhelpful pressure to expect ourselves to always be
on top of things – and it means we project a less than truthful,
overly positive persona in church circles just because we feel we
ought to.

It isn't fair to anyone – those inside *and*
outside of churches – to perpetuate the
myth that Christians have it all together.
Somehow there seems to be a cycle of
having to explain away difficulties, or hide
them, in an effort to make Christianity look
more appealing.

> It isn't fair
> to anyone to
> perpetuate
> the myth that
> Christians have it
> all together.

I can understand why this happens. When preachers are encouraging people to give their lives to Jesus, they use phrases
such as 'He will give you a peace that passes all understanding,'
'He gives you himself as a free gift – his grace is wonderful!' and,
'God's love will set you free.' All of those wonderful statements
are true, but if we emphasize just these points then we give people unrealistic expectations – and basically set them up for disappointment. They need to know the reality of the life they are
choosing and the commitment they are about to make. There is
a cost involved. Jesus never made promises that our lives in this
world would be easy. In fact, he told us quite clearly that, 'In this
world you will have trouble. But take heart! I have overcome the
world' (John 16:33). He also instructed us to take up our crosses
to follow him (see Luke 9:23–5). I find *The Message* translation of
these verses in Luke very interesting:

> Anyone who intends to come with me has to let me lead. You're
> not in the driver's seat – I am. Don't run from suffering; embrace
> it. Follow me and I'll show you how. Self-help is no help at all.

Self-sacrifice is the way, *my* way, to finding yourself, your true self. What good would it do to get everything you want and lose you, the real you?

So embracing suffering and self-sacrifice is the way to find our true selves. No wonder Jesus didn't promise an end to our troubles! It is our attitude towards such difficulties that is important. We don't need to put on a mask to pretend they aren't there, as Jesus himself told us we would have them.

The appeal of authenticity

Why is it, then, that we seem ashamed to tell people the whole picture about life as a Christian? It's almost as if we 'try to compensate for God by presenting our faith as easier than it really is. We cover up the ugliness and hardship of authentic faith,' as Stephen Mattson wrote in an article for *Relevant* magazine.[1] He went on to explain that somehow we seem to be scared of people finding out that our lives are still messy and feel the need to protect God somehow by providing a shiny picture to those looking in.[2]

The truth is, God never asked us to cover up the truth about our lives, and he certainly does not need us to protect him on any level. In fact, we are actually dishonouring him when we gloss over reality. When we try to pretend that we aren't feeling a negative emotion such as anguish, we are denying that we *all* have emotions – even God himself.

> When we try to pretend that we aren't feeling a negative emotion such as anguish, we are denying that we *all* have emotions – even God himself.

The Bible shows us that God isn't afraid to feel – and we still view him as perfect, so why do we often feel it isn't okay for us to show our emotions? God expresses how he is jealous for his people (Exod. 34:14), is deeply troubled (Gen. 6:6), feels anger and hatred towards those who are wicked (Ps. 11:5–6). We also see Jesus experiencing a full range of human emotions. We've talked about him being honest with his disciples when he was overwhelmed with grief, but, for example, it was his righteous anger that caused him to drive out the money lenders from the temple (see Matt. 21:12–13). He was also angry when the Pharisees watched to see if he would heal on the Sabbath so they could accuse him of breaking the Law (see Mark 3:1–6).

If God has revealed his own emotions in the Bible, why do we feel the need to stifle ours? Of course, we can go too far the other way and rely on our feelings rather than God, but emotions are like signposts into what is going on deeper within ourselves and we would do well to take note of them.

One of the most beautiful things about churches is that they are *supposed* to be full of honest people who are willing both to be authentic about their struggles and to learn how to stand by one other and accept help and direction from God and each other. (See Acts 2:42–47 and 4:32–35 – the early church met and prayed together every day, and ensured there were no needy amongst them, so they must have been honest about their needs.)

Thinking about it, wouldn't that actually be incredibly – *appealing* to outsiders looking in? As Sarah Walton says, in *Hope When It Hurts*: 'The world doesn't need to see more people who seem to have it all together; it needs to see real people with real struggles, real emotions, and a real hope.'[3]

Years ago I was really encouraged by something that a work colleague said to me. As I have said, I am someone who cannot hide when I'm hurting, but I also hadn't hidden that I am a Christian. Rather than trying to paint a picture of a glorious and victorious life, I simply and quietly got on with my life and was open about where I was at while chatting to colleagues. This particular person said to me that my attitude, and the way I was 'real' about the difficulties I experienced in life, had made him rethink his opinion of Christians. Today, too, as I spend time with mums from school, sharing in their pain when they are facing hard situations, and being honest when I am too, I am convinced I am building bridges with them, rather than putting them off my faith.

Being shaped and moulded

As we have seen, the Bible makes it clear that we will each face difficulties – but it also reassures us that God is trustworthy and he uses them to shape and mould us (see Rom. 5:3–5). In his commentary on Revelation Phil Moore asserts that if we feel we can blame God for the suffering in the world, then we must also concede that he is big enough to trust when we are suffering ourselves.[4] Jesus didn't shy away from suffering himself while on earth, so it isn't as if he remains distant when we endure difficulties. His suffering ultimately means that he will lead us to a place without suffering one day. I am encouraged by this verse: 'For the joy that was set before him he endured the cross, scorning its shame, and sat down at the right hand of the throne of God' (Heb. 12:2). Set in the context of verses about us persevering, I believe it is reminding us, partly, that Jesus found strength to face the cross by reflecting on the redemption that he would be providing for us.

When we suffer we can have the tendency to cry out to God for deliverance. There is nothing wrong with that, and it is important to bring that deep cry to him, but how often do we ask him if there is something he wants to teach us through the pain? How often do we ask if there is someone he wants us to reach out to through it? How often do we simply submit humbly to him and say, 'Not my will, Lord, but yours be done' even when we cannot understand the purpose behind our suffering?

I do believe God wants us to get to the same place as the psalmist, who was able to say:

> I desire you more than anything on earth.
> My health may fail, and my spirit may grow weak,
>> but God remains the strength of my heart;
>> he is mine forever . . .
> how good it is to be near God!
>> I have made the Sovereign LORD my shelter (Ps. 73:25–28 NLT).

Perhaps, instead of trying to hide our difficulties – from others and even ourselves – we should sit with them for a while. So often we can absorb unsaid messages telling us that we simply need to give everything to God, pick ourselves up and claim Jesus' victory for our lives. (Note the 'pick ourselves up' – that's a key, as it reveals this is something we try to do in our own strength.) But that can minimize what we have been through, and we can learn not to deal with things openly and properly.

Rather than being overly dramatic (which is another unhelpful way people can view others' response to pain), sitting honestly in acknowledgement of our suffering and/or struggles is a legitimate part of the process. When we openly admit that we are suffering and there is nothing we can do to stop it, we start to move away from self-sufficiency and towards God. And we need to understand that he doesn't always simply take the suffering away. It can actually be a gateway to getting closer to him, which we would miss otherwise. Psalm 34:18 says: 'The LORD is close to

> Suffering can actually be a gateway to getting closer to him, which we would miss otherwise.

the broken-hearted and saves those who are crushed in spirit.' He comes near to us, desires to heal our inner beings – and promises to walk through the process of healing with us.

The Japanese art form Kintsugi can be useful when think-ing about how God actually uses our brokenness and pain. The Bible says that 'we have this treasure in jars of clay' (2 Cor. 4:7) and that God is the one who fashions us, the clay: 'We are the clay, you are the potter; we are all the work of your hand' (Isa. 64:8). Kintsugi is the specialized method of repair-ing broken pots and other ceramics with a special lacquer that is mixed with precious metal (gold, silver or platinum). This holds the broken pieces back in place together and, the wonderful thing is, the repaired item is viewed as even more desirable than the original.

I love that image, as it speaks to me about what God has done in my own life. He has particularly used the hardest, most broken parts of my past (yes, even those that were due to my own mistakes and sins) to reach out to others. As I have hum-bled myself before him, repented and then allowed his heal-ing to come, he has redeemed them and made them beautiful through that process. His glory has shone through my weakness. *That* is the message of hope and grace that I believe we should be speaking to one another. That being a new creation does not mean ignoring what we have been through – or disregarding our present difficulties – rather it is that sense of allowing God's transformation power to be at work in our lives.

Giving each other permission

God never tells us that we need to be ashamed of whatever we are going through or hide it from other people. He's given us community for a reason – to reveal God's love to those around us through the way that we care for one another. Each one of us needs that helping hand, as life is tough! I do realize that we need to have close friendships in which we share our burdens, rather than splurging all our struggles and difficulties to the possible stranger sat next to us in church (see Chapter 16). However, I also think we need to learn, as churches, to allow space within our congregational gatherings for people to lament – and simply to voice that suffering is an inevitable part of being a Christian.

It saddens me that, in an effort to acknowledge the freedom that Jesus won for us, sometimes we can gloss over or totally ignore the everyday problems that we face. As someone who leads times of corporate worship, I understand that when we come together on a Sunday we want to lift people's eyes off their circumstances and onto God. We need to be encouraging one another to praise him in every circumstance – as Paul did (see Acts 16:25). And yet we need to be real as we do so and allow space for people to express their pain before God as well as their praise.

It isn't just in corporate sung worship times either. Very rarely do we hear preaching about the glory there is to be found in suffering. But our perfect example, Jesus, was the 'suffering servant'. Our own sufferings give us the opportunity to relate to him more closely. And, as we have seen, he also showed us that it is okay to express our pain. The short- est verse in the Bible is 'Jesus wept' (John 11:35) – he felt the pain of losing his friend Lazarus, even though he knew that he would soon be raising him from the dead.

> The beautiful way that God weaves our lives together through the tapestry of pain, as well as laughter, should be celebrated – not stifled.

I realize that we can all find it hard to ex- plain certain aspects of life, and so we may shy away from exploring those. Yet the beautiful way that God weaves our lives to- gether through the tapestry of pain, as well as laughter, should be celebrated – not stifled. Yes the process is painful, but it is through Jesus that we are healed, and he faced the ultimate act of suffering on the cross. Our very salvation came through the wounds of Christ: 'he was pierced . . . he was crushed . . . by his wounds we are healed' (Isa. 53:5).

Acknowledging the mystery

Because we so often simply don't understand it, we tend to view suffering as having a cause and effect – that it is the result of sin. While it *can* be, at times, it certainly isn't always. It is detrimen- tal to us, and those around us, if we always try to find a reason when we – or someone close to us – suffers.

God invites us to wrestle with him over the harder things we encounter in our lives. I love the image in Genesis 32:22–32 of Jacob wrestling with God, because there is a real intensity and purpose there. Jacob persisted in his struggle all night. I used to think he was so impertinent for doing so, but now I realize

God came down to him and engaged with him – and was happy to do so! What we have to accept, however, is that he won't always give us a satisfactory answer to all our questions,[5] because we have limited understanding compared to his: 'Who has known the mind of the Lord? Or who has been his counsellor?' (Rom. 11:34). I think that is one of the reasons that the book of Job is included in the Bible.

Job had done nothing wrong but still endured immense suffering. His immediate response, on first hearing about his children's death was incredible: 'At this, Job got up and tore his robe and shaved his head. Then he fell to the ground in worship' (Job 1:20). His friends, too, began by supporting him well:

> They set out from their homes and met together by agreement to go and sympathise with him and comfort him. When they saw him from a distance, they could hardly recognise him; they began to weep aloud, and they tore their robes and sprinkled dust on their heads. Then they sat on the ground with him for seven days and seven nights. No one said a word to him, because they saw how great his suffering was (Job 2:11–13).

However, they then tried to make sense of what was happening, and began to suggest that perhaps Job was not as upright as he seemed to be. Has that ever happened to you? In the midst of suffering, have those close to you tried to find a valid reason – and ended up hurting you in the process? That has certainly happened to my mum. Well-meaning church members have spoken things over her which simply heaped more condemnation onto her already desperately hurting heart . . .

Sometimes there simply is no understandable reason for the bad things we go through. God rebuked Job's friends for trying to explain away Job's suffering, as they had become critical. They also made a lot of false assumptions in the process, which revealed they did not truly understand the character of God (see Job 42:7). When we are walking alongside a friend, we need to be careful not to put words into God's mouth as it were. It is far more important to give one another space and simply to be there for each other.

Praising through the pain

Making space to acknowledge our difficulties was something I really felt God pressing upon me to do last year. When I prayerfully considered what the subject of our church women's event was to be, I felt him direct me to the subject of 'Praising Through the Pain'. I was drawn to ask three different women to speak, each of whom had taught me much about staying faithful throughout difficulties. They included my mother, who lives with constant physical pain and also the emotional pain of having a husband who continues to reject God. The other two are dear friends – both have experienced miscarriages, one is in great pain daily and the other has suffered a lot of grief and loss in her family. Each one of them refuses to give up on their faith, and continues to worship God every day, while being honest about their difficulties too.

That event included much laughter, and a lot more tears, but what it did most of all was give the women in our church a deeper understanding of one another. (Many people came up to me afterwards and commented that they would never have thought that those women had been through so much.) It also gave us all 'permission' to be more open with one another.

There was a general space that day to praise God as well as voice the pain and hurt together. The one song that really hit home during that time (and one that I think has such popularity precisely because of the way it reaches hearts wherever they are at) was Matt Redman's '10,000 Reasons'. That song declares a determination to praise God whatever each day brings, right through until the day we draw our last breath.

God truly is a God who works all things 'for the good of those who love him, who have been called according to his purpose' (Rom. 8:28) – even if it takes us a lifetime to see it. We may not ever see it fully in our lifetimes. Those heroes of faith listed in Hebrews 11 didn't actually experience the promises of God for themselves. Scripture tells us: 'All these people were still living by faith when they died. They did not receive the things promised; they only saw them and welcomed them from a distance' (Heb. 11:13). That truly is faith isn't it? Learning to hang on and live a faithful life, believing God's promises even when we don't see the fullness of them in our lifetime, is a journey I think God longs to take us all on. Let's refuse to accept theology that doesn't allow space for difficulties, and allow God to draw us closer to himself in our times of pain.

Personal reflection

- Do you have a safe place within your church community where you feel you can be honest about your struggles? If so, thank God for it. If not, what changes do you think need to happen? Is there any way you can make a start by being that safe place for others? What would that look like?

- Spend some time reflecting on the idea of our lives being like Kintsugi (you may like to look up a picture of a Kintsugi pot – try the Kintsugi gallery at www.lakesidepottery.com if so). Then think about how God has used suffering in your own life to shape and mould you into a more beautiful creation.

- Do you ever wrestle with God? If so, is it something that deepens your faith? If you have never done so, how could you bring some of the more perplexing parts of your life before him today?

13

The Mask Becomes Our Identity

We can get to a point when we've worn our masks for so long that they can seem to become a part of who we are. We feel more comfortable with them on than we do without them. Our masks truly feel like they *are* our identity, and we can cling to them rather than recognizing that they are, in fact, hiding or distorting our true identity.

Clinging on to what we know

As I've already shared, I spent years wearing a victim mask. It fitted me so well that I got to a point where I couldn't see past it. I couldn't bear the pain of looking beneath it, as the real me felt too vulnerable to be revealed. I think that can often be the reason that we are reluctant to look beneath the mask – because we aren't sure we will like what is underneath. We remember the fears and insecurities that caused us to use our mask as protection in the first place and don't want to face them. We forget that one of God's traits is gentleness, and

> We are reluctant to look beneath the mask – because we aren't sure we will like what is underneath.

that he longs to gently teach us to accept and love ourselves through accepting his love.

I know I was locked into allowing my responses to situations and circumstances to be directed by the victim mentality I had allowed to take hold of me. Even after I had, for the most part, broken free from that mindset and mask, I also clung to whatever control I felt I could have. I casually liked to slip on the 'I'm in control' or 'I'm superwoman!' mask so that people couldn't see that, in reality, I was far from in control! I *needed* to know that I could be the self-sufficient, master organizer that I projected outwards to others. That was my protective shell, the one that I used to cover over the vulnerable parts of myself that were still there. But God patiently stripped that all back too. I hadn't realized that my controlling, perfectionist tendencies had crept back into my life and become a problem again long after my original, painful unmasking episode. That is, until a moment in our small group . . .

We hosted and led a small group meeting in our home every week, and one evening someone spilt a drink on our floor. Pretty much everyone jumped up to find a cloth to clean up the mess, out of fear of my response. I was horrified and asked gingerly, 'Am I really that bad?' To my embarrassment people honestly explained that yes, I was. Although I was mortified at the time, I was glad that God used my friends to highlight an area of myself that I needed to let go.

The massive, life-changing moment that God used to begin shaping this part of me was when I became a mum. Being someone who was a control freak, I certainly freaked out when my children were babies! I can still remember the feeling of terror when I first took my daughter home from hospital and realized that this young life was totally dependent on me for *everything* – and yet would not stick to my ideas about time-keeping, rules or what was acceptable behaviour. I can laugh about it now – especially as both our children were pretty easy babies (I've since learned). At the time, I plummeted into postnatal depression. I know that I was dealing with a lack of sleep and fluctuating hormones, but I also think my depression was fuelled by a fear of the unknown. I was petrified of being left alone with our children and my whole sense of self was rocked as a result. I didn't realize how much of my identity was still wrapped up in being able to be in control. I felt lost, totally at sea. It was a very painful season.

God taught me a lot during that time, but also graciously allowed me to take small steps. I can remember the feeling of immense satisfaction that swept over me when I was able to do my first batch of ironing a few weeks after our daughter was born. That seems quite ridiculous to me now but was so important at the time. You see, I hate ironing, but I like to feel that I'm being the best wife and mother I can be, and part of that is providing clean and ironed clothing (although I'm not so fussy about ironing *everything* these days). But, before I got to the point of being able to tackle the ironing myself, God took me through the journey of allowing others to do it for me. Even now, I have some wonderful friends who insist on doing my ironing when they can see my schedule is overwhelming. While I can sometimes still wrestle with feeling embarrassed, I am coming to realize that accepting help is not a weakness; it is a way that God chooses to show his love to me through other people, as well as growing my character in the process. While I *do* still like to be on top of these things, I no longer find my sense of identity or self-worth in them.

God also graciously changed our circumstances quite dramatically – and I didn't appreciate it initially. My husband was still a record producer when our daughter was born, but the record company he was working for relocated, which meant he lost his permanent job, as there was no studio where they had moved to. I had just given up work to have our child (I was already freelance), so there was no income from me – and suddenly he had none either. It meant we had to trust God financially, which caused an extra worry (particularly for me). However, it did give me the wonderful gift of Steve next to me while I navigated the difficult time of working out how to do life with a small child. There were moments when he simply took over and led the way, which was exactly what I needed. It allowed me space to heal emotionally, but it also taught me that I am not always the one with all the answers. And that's okay.

I had always assumed I would be a capable, organized mum, but right from the start of two difficult pregnancies (filled with sickness) and the heartache of having to give up breastfeed-ing, I learned that I could do nothing in my own strength. It just wasn't working! It was all out of my control; I simply *had* to lean into God just to make it through each day. A hard lesson, but a vital one that has, over the years, helped me to open myself up to whatever adventure God has for me each day, rather than being tied into a list of 'oughts' and 'shoulds'. I have had seasons of being better at this than others, but God has continued to teach me.

One of the most recent suggestions that has really helped me has been praying each morning for God to order my day. It has allowed me to hold less rigidly to my own ideas for what I want to achieve, and opened me up to the opportunities God may have for me. Over and over again, I have found that he has so graciously provided me with the inspiration and time to fit in the work that needs to be done each day.

The fear of letting go

I know that I am not alone; there is a ten-dency in so many of us that wants to stick with what we know rather than let go of the masks that are being used to hide and protect the more vulnerable us under-neath. Sometimes our masks are based on

> Whatever the mask is, it becomes almost like a comfort blanket to us.

some truly awful experiences, and yet to let them go feels like we would be losing a part of ourselves and so we continue to cling to them. Whatever the mask is, it becomes almost like a comfort blanket to us.

I have spent time supporting people who have systematically worked through the pain of past experiences, but hold back at the point of completely letting go because they are scared. They are worried about who they might be once the identity they had from those traumas has gone, because so much of them-selves seems to be tied up in them. And that's understandable, when our sense of self is made up of not only the characteristics we were born with but also the circumstances in which we were brought up and things we have experienced over the years (see Chapter 5).

However, the Bible tells us, 'Therefore, if anyone is in Christ, the new creation has come: the old has gone, the new is here' (2 Cor. 5:17). That doesn't mean that God completely wipes out who we were before we accepted Jesus. He is not intent on get-ting rid of the unique personality traits and passions that each of us has; after all, he placed them inside of us in the first place when he knitted us together in our mother's womb. Psalm 139 says 'you created my inmost being' (v.13). He knows us inside out, but he also wants us to be free enough to enjoy what it

means to be his children. That may well include, as I have found, redeeming difficult
experiences so that they no longer negatively shape our core identity but, rather,
enrich the way that we can reach out to
others. An image I have found helpful to
explain this concept of old and new is that

> He knows us
> inside out, but he
> also wants us to
> be free enough
> to enjoy what it
> means to be his
> children.

of a caterpillar turning into a butterfly. The basic elements that
made up the caterpillar originally (that is, its genes) are still there
and yet it has been utterly transformed into something far more
stunning. God does the same with our lives, transforming us to
reflect the beauty of Jesus.

I acknowledge that it can be hard to give up the old and familiar, but that can be because we are clinging to a sense of
security in the protective covering we've worn for so long. To
continue with the image of the caterpillar, it is almost as if we
can get stuck at the cocoon stage – we sense that God is wanting us to undertake a transformation but we don't feel able to
break out into that and so remain wrapped up tightly in the familiar layers that we've built up around ourselves.

If we *can* learn to trust God, as we have seen before, it is
in him that we find true security. We may have been used
to being the protector of our hearts, but he could be lovingly leading us to let go of a self-protective layer that we
no longer need, as he wants us to allow *him* to be our protection. As the psalmist discovered: 'The LORD is my rock, my
fortress and my deliverer; my God is my rock, in whom I take
refuge, my shield and the horn of my salvation, my strong-
hold' (Ps. 18:2).

I remember when Elizabeth first joined the church. We spent
time together praying and working through some issues from

her past, and she experienced the sense of not wanting to let go. So I've asked her to share her story:

In my teenage years, I suffered abuse at the hands of my then fiancé. I had freely made the decision to put God second and my relationship first but, as the relationship unfolded, I found my identity and security in who I was being slowly chipped away. I felt too ashamed to speak to anyone, sure that they would not believe me. I also remember feeling so guilty, as it had been my choice to pursue a relationship that I knew was wrong in God's eyes. Rather than allowing myself to be vulnerable, I built a wall and locked all the shame, anger and hurt inside. Occasionally it would bubble over; there were times when I threw punches at complete strangers, threw plates across a room and pulled out my own hair. When the relationship ended, I remember a feeling of immense relief, yet I still did not let my guard down and talk about what had really happened and what I was feeling on the inside. My robotic, 'I'm fine, really well, thank you,' response to any questions about how I was continued for years.

God was very gracious to me, and eventually led me to a church in which people had the time, patience, grace and confidence to challenge me and support me in working through what were, at times, overwhelming emotions. I found the process terrifying, as the anger, hurt, shame and guilt had been part of who I was for so long that I didn't know what would happen if I was to let them go. I was scared I would lose part of myself and was unsure what would fill their place if I let those emotions go. They had become such a crutch for me that it was impossible to imagine life without them. God was very patient with me but, ultimately, I needed to make the decision to let them go for myself. He wouldn't take them from me until I had offered them up.

By surrendering the parts of me that were basically rotten, in exchange God offered me a freedom, healing and peace that I had never known before. It wasn't a one-stop journey; years later God still reveals his love to me and is still working through the hurts and scars I carry. Yet if I had not let God in, if I had not let down my guard and allowed other people to minister to me and come alongside me, then I would not have been able to fully receive God's message of hope and his redemptive love.

Recognizing our core beliefs

The principle of loss and gain underpins the way the world works. We can see that in the way plants allow their flowers and leaves to die right back, only for new ones to emerge in the springtime. A study of 100 centenarians looked at how well they were dealing with the process of growing old. The ability to adapt to loss, to let go, was one of the specific ways cited.[1] I am convinced that there is, in fact, a necessary letting go in every part of our lives at times. Regarding our mask-wearing tendencies, if we learn to let go of the things (lies, past pain and so on) that cause us to wear masks, we are then able to be more open to receive (or gain) positive things from God. Letting go was certainly something God wanted to teach me, as I explain below.

One of the things I have found so helpful myself, and when working with others, is to understand the role of ungodly beliefs. These are things that we have based our sense of self on that are simply untrue, but we've allowed our whole persona to grow up around them. They have, in effect, helped to 'create' our masks. One of mine, which you may have guessed already, was that my value was in what I did rather than in who I was. It helped to create that need in me to always be seen as capable and organized. I didn't recognize it until I undertook some counselling and some gentle probing enabled me to express some of the core beliefs I held, but had never voiced before. The counsellor and I then looked to see if each belief matched up to what God's Word says and, if it didn't, we worked on a godly belief that I would meditate on daily to facilitate a change in my thinking. For example, to counter the belief that my value is in what I do, I meditated on the following:

> As God heals my heart, I shall believe more and more that the Father designed me just as I am for his pleasure. I am delightful to him.

I can still remember the picture that the counsellor saw at the same time: she said she could see me as a little snowflake, enjoying 'dancing' or floating around. A snowflake is tiny and yet it is incredibly intricate and beautiful. Recollecting that picture over the years has been such a helpful reminder of how much I am loved, how much care God put into creating me and that I can also relax and just enjoy 'being'.

If you recognize a tendency in yourself to cling on to a protective mask, but aren't sure why you do so, prayerfully consider if there are core beliefs you hold that are causing you to avoid letting go (it may be helpful to do this with a friend or counsellor).

The difference between masks and roles

I recognize that there may be particular situations in which we feel we have no choice but to wear a mask of sorts. Perhaps there is a need for a 'professional front' in the job environment we work in (I've already mentioned how introverted artists need to become extroverts to showcase their work to the world). Some workplaces can be quite competitive, so there is a need to be louder than perhaps comes naturally in order to push ideas forward and be heard. I would still argue that this is often workplace culture, rather than necessity, and that a different type of leadership can be modelled. As someone who is quieter, I find 'loud' working environments difficult – and possibly unnecessary a lot of the time. There are many successful business people who do not fit the cliché of being boisterous and pushy. In *Quiet*, Susan Cain reminds us that many of the great CEOs of our time aren't naturally loud. She asserts that some of their more introvert qualities, such as sensitivity and taking time to think before speaking, should be celebrated and harnessed much more than they are currently.

Having said that, perhaps you are a boss or project leader in your workplace and people are looking to you constantly for direction. In such environments, there can be a pressure to wear a mask occasionally in order to become the person people are looking to. You may feel you can't show your vulnerable side very often – perhaps it isn't viewed as appropriate, nor would it help those around you. And you might actually find it easier to manage staff if you are projecting a particular persona – or at least emphasizing a particular aspect of yourself while hiding other parts. The same can be true within other professions: if you are a teacher, you may need to project positivity and enthusiasm, even when you don't feel that way, so your students remain engaged. And people such as receptionists and newsreaders need to give off an air of professionalism that may necessitate hiding personal feelings. As a hairdresser, you can be a friendly listening ear to your clients but you still need to keep focused on the job at hand, which can mean shutting yourself off from your own emotions.

If you have been wearing a mask of 'professionalism' all week, it can be incredibly difficult to suddenly take it off and relax, and just 'be', without agenda. The 'real you' can seem somewhat alien as you've lived with your 'other persona' for the majority of the week. This can result in carrying over this persona when relating to friends and other church members, which isn't appropriate. I've seen this happen, when people are so used to speaking to others in a particular way at work, but then they use the same techniques at church and come across as bossy, fake or detached. This is because church is family; when we are a bunch of volunteers working together, we don't need to put up fronts with one another. We need mutual respect and love – things I would argue are helpful in the workplace too.

There may be a need for you to ask God to help you unwind from a week at work, to enable you to feel comfortable enough to reveal the whole of yourself to him and those close to you. However, I do believe it is important, also, to learn how to differentiate between what is actually you and what is simply a role you are currently fulfilling.

To understand this a little further, I know that as a mother I have a particular role. I can't keep breaking down in front of my children whenever I find an aspect of motherhood difficult. I need to be strong – for them – and often I discover that I am a lot stronger than I ever thought I was. I also am learning, as my daughter is getting ever closer to teenagehood, that there are moments when it is right to share my struggles with her, as it helps her understand her own. But, while I may uncover more about who I truly am through the role of motherhood, it is not *all* I am.

It is the same with the times when I speak – or have meetings with publishers. I am in such a privileged position as an introvert freelancer, in that I can focus on my writing without distraction, at home – in my pyjamas if I want to! But I can't be as laid-back when I am doing those other parts of my job that take me outside of the home. There needs to be a level of professionalism in the way that I present myself.

There is a distinct difference between the roles that we undertake in our lives, and the masks that we wear. The roles change over the years, and they give us experiences that reveal parts of our true selves. But we need to hold on to these roles lightly, as they do evolve – and sometimes end. So, as a mother I need to be able to let go of my children when they have grown their wings and it's time for them to fly. And while they are still with me, I need to remember that they are a gift from God to be held lightly, not clung to so tightly I suffocate the things God is birthing in them as individuals.

If we hold a particular role at work, it isn't all we are. We may change jobs before too long, so we need to make sure that we do not hold on too tightly to that role. The difficulty comes when we view our role as our identity. Our culture makes it seem the natural thing to do though, as so much value is placed on what we do. But this could mean we are setting a role up as an idol in our lives, as we begin to look to it, rather than God, to find our security and self-worth.

Perhaps people become workaholics, never wanting to retire, because they aren't sure of who they are without their role at work. That role may have become the mask they are hiding behind. The sad thing is, their true self may well have become, as Linda Douty describes it, 'an orphaned child – unknown, unloved and unnurtured'.[2] So, even if we feel we have to adopt a mask temporarily, it is important that we recognize that for what it is, rather than allowing our identity to begin to grow up out of it. Reminding ourselves that we are, first and foremost children of God – loved, accepted and adopted by him, regardless of any roles we fulfil in the home, at work and at church – is a vital way of keeping ourselves away from of the trap of viewing our masks as our real selves.

My mum has had a much more extreme experience of having to let go of roles than many of us will. Forty years of battling with lupus and rheumatoid arthritis, as well as other illnesses, has forced her to give up much, and she has had times of despair as she's come to terms with what it means for her. I've asked her to explain:

My medical problems have robbed me of so much over the years. I've had to give up careers that I had embarked on, my love of the outdoors, especially walking regularly with my husband and our walking group; entertaining – I was always a keen cook involved in catering for weddings, parties and so on. Gardening was a shared passion with my husband; now I just watch. Gradually all my household chores have been taken away too. I've always even enjoyed the ironing, but now I have a wonderful 'treasure' who comes in and takes care of the house, including the ironing, because I no longer can.

This has all, at times, made me wonder what use I am to anyone – even God. I have also considered whether I am using my illness as a mask occasionally. It's very easy to crawl into my corner of the settee, surrounded by all that I need – books, Bible, puzzles, phone, pencils, writing paper – and pass the days away. Because of the tremendous amount of medication that I take, I do sleep a lot too.

I don't have a problem now with being rather than doing – but that is something that, ultimately, I've had very little choice with. I can do so little that I've had to learn that I am valuable to God just for being here.

I'm often more aware of his presence than I was when I was fit and well. I can read a Bible passage and then close my eyes and imagine myself in the story with Jesus. This is what heaven will be like, just being with God, enjoying his company, knowing that he asks nothing of me. I can just be his beloved child, as we all are.

Learning to simply be is another journey I think God wants to take us all on. Often we are so busy rushing around, but God wants us to slow down and recognize when we are putting too much emphasis on something we are doing.

If any of the issues raised in this chapter resonate with you, can I gently urge you to work through Chapter 14 slowly and carefully. There I look much more closely at how important truly understanding our identity in Christ is. Through his sacrifice, he made a way for us to become adopted children – and his siblings. It is, therefore, only through him that we are able to stand tall, mask-free and confident in who we are – whatever roles we do or don't have in this life.

Personal reflection

- Can you recognize a tendency in yourself to prefer wearing your mask because it feels safer than not doing so? Why do you think this is?
- Take some time to think about what your core beliefs about yourself are. Prayerfully take them before God (perhaps alongside a friend or counsellor). Are any of them distorted? Do you need to remind yourself of godly truths that can help you replace those distorted ones?
- Have you placed too much of your sense of identity on any of your current roles? Ask God to reveal to you what aspects of your true self those roles have helped you develop, but also to help you hold on to those roles much more lightly.

PART THREE

REMOVING THE MASK

'In order to know who we are, we need to draw close to the one who knows us better than we know ourselves.'

Lucy Mills, *Forgetful Heart*[1]

'Self-sacrifice is the way, my way, to finding yourself, your true self. What good would it do to get everything you want and lose you, the real you?'

Jesus in Luke 9:25, *The Message*

I know how overwhelming it can be to start to reveal the true you beneath the mask. As I've shared earlier, it was one of the most painful parts of my journey – but also the most freeing. One of the best encouragements we have for this process is remembering who God says we are. The problem is, we can have a tendency to look to the wrong places to find out our identity – often coming to God and his Word last. And, if we are being honest, it can be difficult to *truly* believe what the Bible says about our identity. However, it is so important that we take time to immerse ourselves in what the Bible teaches us – both through the messy lives of people who weren't perfect and what Jesus and the disciples taught.

PART THREE

REMOVING THE MASK

Remember Who You Are

So many of the reasons for mask-wearing that we've explored are rooted in issues with our identity. For example, why is it that we are so scared of people knowing that perhaps things aren't going so well for us, or we are struggling with a particular issue? As we have seen, this can be such a natural, subconscious response for many of us but, when we pare it right back, it boils down to us making our fear of others bigger than our fear of God. We are so worried about what people might think of us, and how they might respond – how they might treat us once they realize we aren't perfect. It makes us forget that God already knows us inside and out and also knows everything we are dealing with at any one moment.

And he accepts us. Totally. Utterly.

Actually, God does more than just accept us. He loves us. Unconditionally.

As we have seen, God's love for us is not based on what we do, how well we 'perform'. If only we could accept that fully, and yet, how many of us have truly accepted *everything* God says about our identity in him?

Sometimes it can seem too simple to be true, especially for those of us living in an over-sophisticated society. But the truth is he loves us and accepts us. That's it. No 'but', no 'if only'. And sometimes it just seems downright outrageous. He has adopted us into his family and given us the same inheritance as his son, Jesus, whom he sent to the cross to die for our sin so that we could enjoy that inheritance. Romans 8:16–17 tells us: 'The Spirit himself testifies with our spirit that we are God's children. Now if we are children, then we are heirs – heirs of God and co-heirs with Christ.'

That really is pretty incredible!

And yet, even if we believe that that is true, rather than being most concerned by what our heavenly Father thinks of us, so often we live as if we care more about the opinion of the person standing next to us. Somehow we get our perspectives all skewed. We need to learn to stop looking to others for validation, and spend more time gazing on our Father's face, which is full of his love, grace and mercy.

> We need to learn to stop looking to others for validation, and spend more time gazing on our Father's face.

Jesus walked closely with the Father, knowing his approval at all times. He knew who he was, which is how he was able to say, 'not my will but yours' even when he faced the horrors of the cross. His assurance of his identity was evident right from an early age – take the incident in Luke 2 in which his parents were returning home after the Festival of the Passover and discovered that he was not with them. They spent three days searching, only to find him in the temple courts. When they reprimanded him his response was, 'Didn't you know I had to be in my Father's house' (v.49). If only our sense of identity and purpose was as strong!

Having a wobble

I'm talking to myself about this as I write these words. My journey through my teenage years and during the early years of our
marriage has made me passionate about seeing others come to
the place of knowing their security and self-worth is best found
in God. I write about this subject, I preach it – some would say
I must be an expert in it! And yet . . .

During these last few weeks, I have had a reminder that I can
still take my eyes off where my identity lies. I've had a really difficult situation in which I have felt hurt, overlooked, belittled
and ignored – and it's really crumpled my self-esteem. I've been
shocked at the force of my response, which I think may have
been heightened by my daughter going through something
similar. I've watched her, hurt for her, tried to comfort her; but
then I realized that I was so broken myself by what happened
that I just *had* to be honest with her about my own hurt feelings.

It all affected me so much. I was disappointed in myself for
'failing' yet again – so I wrestled with God about it. I asked him
to show me why, when I thought I had this identity stuff 'sorted',
I could be so rocked to the core again. I had to admit to myself that
part of it is that longing to be noticed, to be affirmed by others.
While I know God is ultimately the one in whom my value lies, it is
so easy to be distracted by those that are physically in front of me.
To look to the people I see day in, day out to give me validation.

One of the beautiful things that has come out of these difficult weeks is how I've been journeying more intimately with
my daughter. It's made us much closer, and I think admitting
I didn't have all the answers, that I was hurting too, helped that
happen. She had shut down, but when I was open with her she

slowly began to open up just a little. So I then went on to share with her each day how I was feeling, how I was taking those emotions to God and asking for his help. We talked about forgiveness, about turning the other cheek. I openly admitted to her that I don't always get this issue right, but that I am praying that she will learn to find her security and self-worth in God at a far earlier age than I did.

These last few weeks have also reminded me of how we can have an inbuilt capacity to put ourselves down. Even though I don't think I was the cause of what happened, I immediately started searching inside myself, convinced that the problem lay with me rather than anyone else. Why is it that so often we struggle to be compassionate towards ourselves? My husband and close friends had to say to me that I am still cherished by them and that I needed to lay down the need to know why, the need to try to fix things, and just let go. Slowly, through journaling, prayer, soaking in particular Bible verses and talking things through, I learned to put my focus back on God.

'In Christ': the key

I don't know if you remember the interesting exercise when a skin care manufacturer hired a forensic sketch artist to draw women as they described themselves. He then drew the same women using descriptions from a complete stranger. (These are known as real beauty sketches.) The differences between the two were very telling, as the women always described themselves more negatively. Standing in front of the two sketches, comparing them both, was a powerful and emotional moment for the women.[1]

The slogan for this campaign was: 'You're more beautiful than you think'.

But, of course, as we are looking at remembering who we are, it's about the whole person, which is of far more importance than outward appearance, because:

> God says *in Christ* you are stronger than you think you are . . .
> You are more powerful than you think . . .
> You are more loved than you think . . .
> You are more forgiven than you think . . .
> You are more secure than you think . . .

The key is recognizing it is only 'in Christ' that we have all these things. Through him we are now clothed in his righteousness, and have the mind of Christ (1 Cor. 2:16). This is such an important truth that God's Word uses the phrase 'in Christ' 86 times!

But why do we find it so hard to accept who God says we are?

Arianna Walker is the Chief Executive of Mercy UK, which works with girls aged 18–28 who are struggling with life-controlling issues. In her book *Mirror Image* she explains how she has seen first-hand how many of us base our identity on what others have said or done to us or on big events and issues that we have had to deal with, such as abuse, bullying or loss.[2] Our past and the way people have treated us in it can not only cause us to wear masks, but it can also block us from accepting what God says about our identity.

The problem is, as we have already explored, we naturally and subconsciously respond to what has happened to us and what other people have said and done to us. But if we continue to feed our identity out of such things, we end up with

a distorted view. We can become self-attacking, always viewing ourselves negatively, blaming ourselves for everything
and not accepting love and kindness from anyone – least of
all God.

A friend of mine, who has been a Christian for many years
(and who I would say is very secure in who she is), sat under
the negativity of a boss who simply didn't like her voice. As a
teacher, she uses her voice constantly, but her headteacher intimated that she was ineffective in her role simply because she
didn't like listening to her. There was nothing wrong with what
my friend was doing in the classroom; she worked hard every
day and in fact is known for her creativity and for engaging well
with children. However, having had that lie drip-fed to her for
years she began to believe it. The result was that it crushed her
confidence and caused deep pain. As God began to show her
how it was robbing her, and was also beginning to affect other
areas of her life, she chose to open up, admit how the lie had
had such a big hold on her and then cut it off, refusing to allow it
space any longer. She took time to soak in the truth of who God
says she is by allowing her close friends to speak truth over her –
but also through reading the Bible and meditating on relevant
passages for herself.

Turning to God's Word

Drip-feeding lies to us is a way the enemy loves to distract us
from the truth, be it through our culture, relationships or other
means. It is *so* important that we combat this by taking time
to feed ourselves with the truths that God's Word tells us and
choosing to believe them rather than the lies. This takes more

than just a one-off glance through the Bible; it needs to be a systematic, regular reading so that it truly sinks in.

The book of James warns us against a superficial glancing at God's Word, explaining how a deeper interaction with it will change us:

> Do not merely listen to the word, and so deceive yourselves. Do what it says. Anyone who listens to the word but does not do what it says is like someone who looks at his face in a mirror and, after looking at himself, goes away and immediately forgets what he looks like. But whoever looks intently into the perfect law that gives freedom and continues in it – not forgetting what they have heard, but doing it – they will be blessed in what they do (Jas 1:22–25).

I like how this passage infers that if we keep looking at God's Word, looking in the 'mirror' as it were, we then take the truths about our identity away with us and will remember who we are. I know that this takes time and practice. It can be so easy to focus on the reasons why we find it hard to accept who we are in Christ, but by soaking ourselves in God's Word, we *can* start believing what he says about us.

Renewing our minds

What we allow into our thoughts is so important, too. You may think that you cannot control your mind – that whatever pops into your head is subconscious and therefore uncontrollable. But I believe that is yet another lie that our enemy desperately wants us to believe (and puts in an awful lot of effort getting us to), as our minds are often the battlefield for our identities.

Looking back, I can see that I dwelt on the things that people said, or didn't say, to me in recent weeks. I mulled so much over in my mind, wondering what people were doing in those times when I'd been left out. What I did was put *myself* through an unnecessary agony that cost me a lot of tears. When I started refusing to accept those thoughts and focused my mind back on God, I was able to shake off the feelings of unworthiness.

It is hard to reprogramme our minds, but God has told us to 'take captive every thought to make it obedient to Christ' (2 Cor. 10:5). It involves us lining up what we think about (including what we think about ourselves) with what Jesus says. That verse starts by saying 'We demolish arguments and every pretension that sets itself up against the knowledge of God'. It's a very active thing – and we need to persevere with it.

So let's look at an example of how to do this. Perhaps, like me, you have struggled with very low self-esteem. You don't feel

It's about Jesus – he's the key.

that anyone could ever love you. The first step is to recognize that that is not the truth about who you *really* are, because it doesn't line up to what the Bible says: 'But because of *his great love for us*, God, who is rich in mercy, made us alive *with Christ* even when we were dead in transgressions – it is by grace you have been saved' (Eph. 2:4–5, emphasis added). As I've said before, it's about Jesus – he's the key. So, after recognizing the lie, the second step is to choose to turn away from it (repent) and then *realign* our thinking to the truth (as we did with core beliefs in Chapter 13).

My prayer for you (and for myself) echoes what Paul said to the Ephesians:

> I pray that you, being rooted and established in love, may have
> power, together with all the Lord's holy people, to grasp how wide

and long and high and deep is the love of Christ, and to know this love that surpasses knowledge – that you may be filled to the measure of all the fullness of God (Eph. 3:17–19).

I know that the above could seem like an over-simplistic, pat answer to anyone who has struggled with issues for a long time. The last thing I would want to do is make a judgement call on anyone. I acknowledge that as human beings there will be things that we need to deal with time and time again in our lives – what's happened to me recently has proved that to me once again. And yet I wholeheartedly believe that grasping hold of God's truth is the way we embrace our true identity.

What stops us?

Romans 12:2 says: 'Do not conform to the pattern of this world, but be transformed by the renewing of your mind.'
   I love how *The Message* version phrases this:

Don't become so well-adjusted to your culture that you fit into it without even thinking. Instead, fix your attention on God. You'll be changed from the inside out. Readily recognize what he wants from you, and quickly respond to it. Unlike the culture around you, always dragging you down to its level of immaturity, God brings the best out of you, develops well-formed maturity in you.

If God's Word holds the truth about who we are, why don't we spend more time meditating on it? Personally, I think it can seem like a very alien thing to do – to read out, memorize and meditate on Scripture that openly challenges our beliefs about ourselves.

It can almost feel a little like the 'name it and claim it' approach that is always overly positive and victorious, never allowing any negativity out of our mouths. In an effort to stay away from the excesses of that, we may have gone too far the other way and just got out of the habit of positively declaring truths over ourselves.

I can certainly relate to that. Over the years I've found loud, demonstrative Christians who've declared things over situations my family has been going through to be overbearing and, at times, downright insensitive. And so I learned to shrink away from anything that seemed remotely like that.

When I first encountered the 'Who I am in Christ' list from the Freedom in Christ course, for instance, I was encouraged to stick it on the fridge and read it out loud each morning.[3] That made me cringe, as to me it felt like brainwashing. And yet, everything on that list is biblical truth that I believe as a Christian. All I was being asked to do was read it out and perhaps learn some of it. It was a useful tool that would help me in coming years, especially in those moments that I have felt low, insecure or worthless. So I chose to bite the bullet and do it even though it felt strange to begin with.

I can wholeheartedly recommend that list of Scriptures. What it shows is that scriptural tools are our weapons to cut down negative thoughts. As Terry Virgo once said, 'It's not mind over matter, it's truth over matter.' We need to do all we can to immerse ourselves in the truth of Scripture. How often, for example, have you muttered under your breath, 'I'm such an idiot' or something similar? When we speak words out we are lining ourselves up in agreement with them, and are, essentially, giving them power. So what we say really does matter.[4] Learning

> Learning to speak the truth of God's Word over ourselves *is* a very powerful thing to do

to speak the truth of God's Word over ourselves *is* a very power-ful thing to do – even if it feels a bit weird to begin with!

Sometimes what God asks us to do seems either too over-whelming or too simple. You might be thinking: read out a few verses? Meditate on them? Learn them? How is that going to help me? And if we don't see instant results, we can cave in and stop trying. And then we moan that God isn't helping us. But, as Peter says in 2 Peter 1:3: 'His divine power has given us everything we need for a godly life through our knowledge of him who called us by his own glory and goodness.'

It is our own personal choice as to whether we believe our identity lies in who God says we are. Even when we choose to do so, sometimes we have to take one lie at a time and replace it with God's truth. It can be a daily fight, in which we each need to determine to take a stand.

Over time, as with any habit, it does get easier. I have cer-tainly found that my *usual* default now, when I find my identity is being questioned in some way, is to turn to the Scriptures I have learned. Yes, I sometimes miss the mark but, even then, God's grace and love gently turn me back to remembering how to take captive those unhelpful thoughts.

Recognizing tactics

It can be useful to regularly remind ourselves that getting us to question our identity is one of the main tactics that the enemy uses against us. He did it right back in the Garden of Eden, get-ting Eve to question God ('Did God really say . . . ?' Gen. 3:1). He also planted the idea in her head that God had told her not to eat the fruit because he didn't want her to become like him (see v.5).

Suddenly the truth of who she was and what God had said was discarded, as she chose to believe the lies that God was actually keeping something from her and limiting her potential as a result.

The devil even tried the same tactic on Jesus! Interestingly, during his baptism, God spoke affirmation over him, 'This is my son, whom I love; with him I am well pleased' (Matt. 3:17). Right after this, Jesus was led into the wilderness and there the devil tempted him, each time using the phrase, 'If you are the Son of God . . .' (see Matt. 4). He tried to question and distort Jesus' identity, but Jesus knew who he was and also knew God's Word, and used both to render the devil's efforts useless.

The devil is predictable and, helpfully, we can see throughout Scripture examples of the tricks he tries to play. It is reassuring to know we are not alone in having our identity questioned by him, and we can learn to recognize his work. Reading about how others overcame (as well as fell prey to) his tactics can arm us with the knowledge we need to stand strong against his attacks on our own identity.

Honest assessment

So, how's your knowledge of God and what he says about you? Do you spend time in the Word studying God's character, as well as his promises about your identity in Christ?

And what feeds your identity daily? How many hours do you spend reading other people's Facebook statuses, looking at how amazing their lives seem to be, or reading glossy magazines looking at 'perfect bodies'? How much time do you spend having your identity fed by truth? Where do you look to find out who you *really* are? Determine right now to start looking in the only place that holds the key to your identity – God's Word.

Personal reflection

Regularly creating my own word cloud/picture based on some of the verses God has drawn me to is a helpful reminder to me of my true identity. Here is a selection you could use to try creating your own (alternatively, feel free to use other truths that God has been speaking to you):

I am chosen (Eph. 1:4) and dearly loved (Col. 3:12), adopted (Eph. 1:5), a new creation (2 Cor. 5:17), holy (Heb. 10:10), clothed in the righteousness of Christ (Isa. 61:10), the apple of [God's] eye (Ps. 17:8), an heir with Christ (Rom 8:17), safe (1 John 5:18), protected (Ps. 91:14), [Jesus'] friend (John. 15:15).

It Takes Courage to Remove the Mask

Being open to the adventure of finding out more about who we truly are beneath our masks gives us the opportunity to develop and grow as people; to become who God intended us to be. We've looked at how soaking ourselves in the truth of who we are in God, through Jesus, is a *huge* part of this process. It gives us the confidence to trust him and let go of clinging to our masks. I acknowledge that this isn't always easy though. For some of us it will take a long time, and the protective layers with which we've covered our true identity will need to be peeled back one by one (perhaps under the gentle guidance of close friends and/or professional counsellors).

I know that the process of removing our masks can be very painful, yet be assured that it is a temporary pain and leads ultimately to our healing. If we keep ourselves closed to God, hiding away beneath our masks year after year, we are causing ourselves a lot more pain – even if we don't realize it. Because keeping a part of

> Keeping a part of ourselves covered blocks us from an intimacy with God that we could otherwise experience.

ourselves covered blocks us from an intimacy with God that we could otherwise experience.

I have indicated that my huge mistakes caused my unmasking to happen all in one go, and I felt vulnerable, ashamed and hurt because of that. I don't believe that is the way that God generally wants to work in us. I refused his gentle leading for a long, long time and it took a crisis for me to actually listen. I like to think of our journey of taking off our masks more like the peeling of an onion. God walks with us and helps us to gently peel off a layer or two. He graciously allows us to pause, and only nudges us again when he knows we are at the right place to peel another layer back. He has certainly done that in my own life, when dealing with my 'I'm in control' mask.

However, even though I am convinced that God works at a pace that is right for each of us as individuals, I realize that it takes courage to take those first steps to remove our masks. So I want us to pause now to look at two wonderful biblical examples of women who were not afraid to reveal who they truly were, at the right time. Our faith is built when we read God's Word, which is why I want to focus on them in this chapter.

Esther: for such a time as this

Whenever I think of mask-wearing, and especially a 'big reveal', it is always Esther that comes to mind. She has taught me a lot about courage, as well as the necessity of counting the cost before removing our masks.

Esther's story is found in the Old Testament in a book named after her. At the start of the book of Esther, we see that King Xerxes was the ruler of Persia, where Esther lived. By this time,

Jewish people enjoyed much freedom in Persia, but not usually in the company of the king! Esther's path crossed the king's because, after his wife Vashti insulted him, he decided to look for a new queen to replace her.

Esther was an orphan, looked after by her cousin Mordecai – who was also Jewish. She must have known a deep sadness in her past, when her parents died or were killed, and yet she didn't allow it to make her bitter. It is encouraging to see how God raised up someone who may have been viewed by others as 'lowly'. As I've experienced through my own situation, God does not overlook those with difficult pasts.

It was customary for the king to simply 'collect' women, who would then be looked after in a harem and expected to wait until the king called for them. So part of the process of finding a new queen involved the king's men searching among the people for women of beauty. Esther was picked out and taken to the palace, but not before Mordecai warned her to hide her true identity.

Not only was Esther keeping back who she truly was, the preparation for seeing the king involved a whole heap of beauty treatments. While this process could be seen as simply enhancing natural beauty, to me it speaks of another mask – which involved focusing purely on outer appearance. Of course, it was her beauty that attracted the king to Esther above all others, and she was made queen.

God's timing

The plot of Esther is full of intrigue, and we can see God's hand at work in the way he ensured people were in the right place at the right time. For example, when Mordecai uncovered a plot to kill the king, both he and Queen Esther, who brought it to the king's attention, found favour in the king's eyes.

But then came the opposition: the king appointed Haman as his right-hand man. When all the other officials except Mordecai bowed down to him, his blood boiled and he vowed to kill all Jews due to Mordecai's offence. He sweet-talked the king into giving him a royal decree allowing him to do so, and Esther then faced a huge dilemma: speak up and risk her own life or keep quiet and see the destruction of the Jewish people in Persia.

This is the crux of the story, and also where Mordecai challenged Esther, as her first response to the horrific news was to say that she could be killed before she even got to implore the king to save her people. It was certainly true that going to the king without being summoned really *was* putting her life in his hands. Unless he extended his golden sceptre to her, she would be killed for entering his presence without permission.

Mordecai spoke directly to her fears, by saying that whether she spoke up or not she would not be saved. This was not a time to bury her head in the sand, but to rise up with courage and reveal who she truly was. Do we have people in our lives who can do the same for us? Challenging us, giving us advice as well as always looking out for us? Mordecai went on to say, 'Who knows but that you have come to your royal position for such a time as this?' (Esth. 4:14). He believed God had brought her to the palace for a particular reason, and encouraged Esther to embrace it.

Esther's response showed courage, wisdom and humility. She listened to Mordecai, agreed to approach the king and asked Mordecai to gather the Jews to pray and fast for her as she prepared. What is so interesting is that she indicated that she would do the same – along with her attendants (Esth. 4:16). Amazingly, even in the palace, where she would have been surrounded by people who were not Jewish, Esther had obviously shared who she truly was with a small group of people. They must have been supportive of her, as she was able to say with confidence that they would also fast and pray. I will return to the subject of having close friends we share most deeply with, in the next chapter.

The big reveal

You can read Esther's full story in the Bible. What I want us to focus on here is the very moment when Esther had to do the big reveal. She had already had to face the king, no doubt with her heart pounding, wondering whether his sceptre would be raised or she would be killed. The fact that he had not called for her for thirty days would no doubt have made her even more nervous at that point (as would the knowledge that Queen Vashti had been disposed of for acting independently). Once the sceptre was held out towards her, Esther simply invited the king and Haman over for a banquet, which gave her and the king time to enjoy one another's company again while keeping her enemy close. During the second banquet she knew that time was running out and she had to finally speak up about who she was.

Imagine how she must have been feeling at that point – facing the most powerful man in the land alongside the one who had vowed to destroy her and all her people. That is a good picture of who we face in our moments of unmasking, too. We are in the presence of our King, but also our enemy (who wants to keep us trapped behind our masks). Fortunately, once Esther revealed that she was a Jew, and that Haman had plotted to kill them all, the king destroyed Haman and the Jews were given permission to defend themselves against any enemies. Esther's unmasking drew love and justice from the king, and saw the enemy thoroughly defeated – and ultimately, we can expect the same from God.

Although there had been very valid reasons for Esther hiding who she truly was, it wasn't until she was open and honest about herself that she was able to fulfil her destiny. I believe that the same is true for us today, and that that is the great promise we can take away from Esther's story. If we will be courageous and ask God to help us remove our masks, we can come into all the fullness that he has for our own destinies (see Chapter 17, where I talk about the unexpected places God has taken me to since removing my mask).

Mary: fixed on Jesus

I wanted to include a story of someone who was able to shun the social 'rules' of her day, to be who she truly was: someone hungry to hear more from her Lord. This is because I know that we face enormous pressures to confirm to our culture today. Society's expectations can be like masks we are being told to wear by our culture. Mary is a great biblical example of someone who refused to wear the masks her society told her she should.

To be honest, I have always been far more drawn to Martha than Mary. I think my tendencies to always be 'doing' have been offended in the past when I've read their story, especially when I get to the part where Jesus told Martha that Mary has chosen 'the better way'. I get quite indignant – surely he must have realized the huge number of chores that needed doing in order for them to host him and his disciples? But in the book study group that I am involved with in our church, we've recently studied *Having a Mary Heart in a Martha World*, and God has challenged me deeply through it.[1] There have been parts of the story that I have noticed afresh – and things I never really saw before.

Mary's story has made me ask myself: how often have I had the courage to fix my eyes on Jesus rather than being distracted by all the jobs and people I may be surrounded by? Those very distractions can be used as 'masks' to hide us from what truly matters – spending time with Jesus and being transformed by him. Perhaps we allow that to happen because we are fearful of sitting totally exposed before God, and so we keep ourselves busy so we can't. I know I can get preoccupied with 'doing', while God simply longs for me to draw closer to him. Of course, it happens when

> Distractions can be used as 'masks' to hide us from what truly matters – spending time with Jesus and being transformed by him.

we allow other people's expectations of us to drive us too. There have been times when I have undertaken acts of service or taken on a particular role because I believed people were expecting me to. I have worn myself out doing so and then realized I have not connected with God in a meaningful way through it. God is gently speaking to me about learning how to serve from a place of rest, going to him first and foremost to be refreshed and find out what he would have me do. As a result, I have become much more interested in Mary as a character. What I find extraordinary, and very challenging, is that each time Mary is mentioned, we see that she doesn't allow her identity to be stipulated by her circumstances.

We first encounter Mary when Jesus visits their home (see Luke 10:38–42). Luke describes Martha as rushing around, being 'distracted by all the preparations that had to be made' (v.40), while Mary 'sat at the Lord's feet listening to what he said' (v.39).

When Martha complained that her sister wasn't helping her, it was a complaint born out of a feeling of injustice – but others could have complained too. For a woman to be sitting with the Teacher, who would have been surrounded by listening men, was abnormal to say the least. I can imagine a few raised eyebrows, certain characters tutting and murmuring amongst themselves that her place was out the back helping her sister, not relaxing with the men. But Mary refused to be confined to the roles of her day – and Jesus applauded her for it. He knew her heart was thirsty to hear more from him, and he didn't mind breaking with tradition in order for that to happen.

Mary was unmarried, which would have held some stigma in those times, as most Jewish girls were promised in marriage by the age of 12. But Mary was living with her brother Lazarus and sister Martha who, interestingly, Scripture suggests owned the house (see Luke 10:38). This may indicate that Martha was a widow. Because the siblings were living together it could mean that their parents had died too, which would have made it more difficult for Mary to find a husband.

What Mary *did* have, however, was half a litre of nard, which was worth around a year's wages. It would certainly have been her most valuable possession, possibly her dowry. So, on a later occasion, when she chose to pour it over Jesus' feet (see John 12:1–3), she was literally giving him her whole life; everything her future was based on. That was it – no masks, no pretences – she was pouring out her whole being in a sacrificial act of love to the one whom she recognized as her saviour. She didn't care what those around her thought. She ignored the gasps that escaped from others' mouths as she had the audacity to let down her hair in public and wipe Jesus' feet with it. She gave no thought either to what her ever-practical sister may say about her extravagance. She just knew this was something she had to do.

And, again, Jesus affirmed her for it . . .

Holy Spirit-inspired courage

Reading about removing masks and reminding ourselves of biblical characters who did so courageously is all very well and good, but the idea of doing the same ourselves can sometimes seem overwhelming. The good news is that this courage is not the kind that we have to muster up for ourselves – it comes from the Holy Spirit who is a gift God has given each of us (see Eph. 1:13–14).

I love the simple truth that church leader and author Phil Moore reminded me of recently: God uses nobodies. As I listened to Phil speak about how clueless the disciples were at times and that even after spending those intense three years with Jesus they often still got it wrong, I was so grateful! Because it means God is willing to use any of us. Fear led the disciples to run and hide when Jesus was arrested. Fear led Peter to disown him too. And yet it was Peter who led the 120 we see at the start of Acts (see Chapter 3 for more on how Jesus taught – and restored – Peter beautifully).

> God uses nobodies.

It was Peter, humble yet bold, who spoke up on the day of Pentecost, completely owning the fact that he was a follower of Jesus. Yet he had been the one who had not long before pretended he had never met him. Yes, God transformed a motley bunch of nobodies, who were full of fear, into courageous ambassadors of his gospel, who were willing to lay their lives down for one another. As we have seen in this chapter, Mary had the courage to look to Jesus for her identity, ignoring others' disapproval when she moved outside of her expected role. And Esther, when preparing to present herself to the king, prayed and fasted, and asked those around her to do the same – no doubt asking for wisdom and courage. We are being offered the same courage today too, if we are willing to humbly submit our whole lives to God.

Personal reflection

Think about what the word 'courage' means for you, and how it relates to your journey with God right now. Perhaps you could jot down your thoughts in a journal?

Do you feel you have the courage to start removing the mask that God has been talking to you about as you've read through this book? If not, could you pray that God would embolden you through his Holy Spirit?

The Support of Friends

In an effort to encourage you to remove your masks, I have been very vulnerable. While at first it was relatively easy to sit and type away about this subject at my desk, speaking about my story on radio and then in front of a sea of faces in church and at women's events has taken a lot of courage. There have been times when I have wondered what on earth I'm doing.

There was one moment when I felt that it was all too difficult, and I couldn't keep laying myself bare like this. I was ready to give up: I didn't yet have a publisher, so I could have just shut the Word file I was writing in and put it away, hidden from sight so no one had to see it. But that day, every time I opened my Bible there were verses about God's people telling their story. I got the message and started writing again, but then I went to that week's worship practice at church and one of the guys commented that he had heard me on the radio and hadn't known what had happened in my past. At that moment I felt exposed – not ashamed, but vulnerable again. But I know in such moments that the end goal is not that feeling of vulnerability, but authenticity before God. And it is those close to me who remind me of God's calling on my life, and of how precious I am to him.

Appropriateness

I am a huge advocate of us being real and honest with one another but I also recognize that in the rush of a quick cuppa and a chat before or after a Sunday meeting we might not always have time to explain how we truly are. And there are times when 'putting it all out there' may not be appropriate. For instance, if I as a worship leader or speaker, or my husband as preacher, stood up each Sunday and told the whole congregation about all the difficult things we'd faced, we would soon pull everyone down. There *is* a place for us explaining what God has taught us through difficult times, but that is not the same as dumping all our 'dirty laundry' on the congregation.

I chatted with the wonderful Cathy Madavan about this. As a leader and a pastor's wife, she believes:

> It is our job as leaders to create a climate and a culture where honesty is encouraged and modelled and where we do real . . . But the goal, at the end of the day, is not 100 per cent honesty, but wisdom. Not all honesty is helpful or appropriate. We all need boundaries and we all need to know where and when and to whom we should bare our souls.

There is such truth in what Cathy has shared. While you may be feeling apprehensive of having to open up to people, I want to reassure you that the level of openness and honesty I believe God is calling us to, can only happen among those we truly trust. I am not advocating sharing with just anyone. Because I know it can lead to pain and

> The level of openness and honesty I believe God is calling us to, can only happen among those we truly trust.

disappointment when we share with people who see our struggles as an opportunity for gossip.

I used to attend a church in which there was a strong prayer
group. But sadly it soon became apparent that the group
seemed to be more intent on gossiping than praying and,
slowly but surely, people stopped sending prayer requests
to them. I also had comments in my survey from people who
were horrified at how other Christians felt it was okay to share
their deepest struggles with others under the guise of prayer
requests. Confidentiality is such an important value to cultivate
within our friendships; without it we can feel betrayed.

Our champions

It is the small group of people to whom we feel that we *can* 'bare
our souls' that I want us to turn our attention to now. They are
the ones who champion us and can help us to be 'real' and authentic. As Cathy mentioned, we need real wisdom in choosing
who we are going to share with on such a deep level. We also
need to feel utterly safe with them before doing so.

Malcolm Down, a publishing colleague, spoke to me about
how a 'men only' small group at his church has given those in
it the space to deepen friendships and be truly honest about
life:

Having attended a male-only home group for three years, I've
found the guys more than willing to open up about all kinds of
issues from addiction to pornography to doubts over marriage
relationships. They would never say so on a Sunday morning but
then, why would they? They have a 'safe place' where they can share

mid-week, but don't feel the necessity to tell everyone so long as their 'trusted mates' know.

It is in our close friendships that we can be honest about the things we struggle with – as well as sharing our greatest high points. I would view Steve as one of my best friends, and in my own home I know I do relax and am truly myself. That means my family see the best – but also the worst – of me. But I know they accept and love me as I am too. There are also friends who I have travelled with over the years, through many situations (both excruciatingly hard and joyful). Some are those who have had to work through the pain inflicted by my foolish mistakes from the past. The great thing, as I said earlier, is that they knew the worst I was capable of, and still chose to love me. Today I serve regularly alongside a friend I have known for over twenty-five years, which is a real joy and privilege. I echo what she says here:

> I value this friendship, because of its honesty, knowing I can be myself – through good or bad times. I know I can be completely honest with Claire and also know she will be honest with me.

Discipling one another

Alongside my long-standing cherished friend, I have made new friends in recent years. I think it is really important to be open to new friendships, and the gifts that God wants to bring to us through them too. I have a friend who I am in a 'discipleship-type' relationship with currently, who has only been in the church for around eight years. When she first came we immediately clicked, and once we had got to know each other better we chose to become 'accountable' to one another. This simply means we are in regular contact via text and email, meet up as often as we can and aren't afraid to ask each other 'difficult' questions.

It is wonderful to have someone I can be totally real with, who invests the time to be in touch regularly throughout the week. She is another person to whom I can admit I am struggling and know she will be praying for me.

There have been awkward moments, when one or other of us has had our feathers ruffled. But I think that is down to our natural self-defence mechanisms kicking in. At the start of this book, I said that I used to stop speaking to people who weren't telling me what I wanted them to. Humility and staying power are vital in accountable relationships, because challenge is hard – we don't like to feel uncomfortable. But it is often in such moments that we grow the most. It is hard to see our own faults, and we need people around us who are willing to gently point out our blind spots to us. They need to be people who we know are totally for us, and who also support and encourage us in our journey of life. They have earned the right to speak into our lives in such a way because of that close connection. It is certainly wonderful to know that my closest friends are determined to see me fulfil my potential in God and do all they can to support me in that.

> Challenge is hard – we don't like to feel uncomfortable. But it is often in such moments that we grow the most.

As I said previously, God has been talking to me about humility recently. It is hard to hear the truth about the uglier sides to my character, but I do want to hear from those friends that I recognize speak wisdom to me. I am choosing to cultivate humility by encouraging myself to go to them and ask for their help and advice – as well as prayer and challenge over things I need to work on. When I read the story of Esther afresh, I was struck by how she not only allowed Mordecai to speak directly into her life (including challenging her), but had also turned to Hegai, the man in charge of the harem, for advice, having recognized his expertise (see Esth. 2:8–9,15). During those times when something in me still seems to resist asking others for their help and/or wisdom, I now remember Esther. I remind myself, too, that being humble is all about positioning myself correctly before God.

Friendship should be safe

I am aware that there will be those of you who have tried being open and honest with certain friends – and have been severely let down by them. Perhaps they have been judgemental and harsh, or maybe they have found what you've shared great 'gossip fodder' and broken your confidence. I know what it can feel like when people hurt you, talk about your struggles behind your back or heap a pile of condemnation on you. If that is the case for you, can I gently suggest, if you haven't already, that perhaps you take some time to work through Chapters 9 and 11 before reading any further.

I do pray that you don't give up on the idea of having close friendships within church. They are meant to be safe, supportive networks. They also give us a chance to be a part of something bigger than ourselves. Just as marriage portrays a wonderful picture of the relationship God has with his bride, I believe godly friendship also allows us to commune more deeply with God and his people, reflecting the unity God desires. When we make ourselves available to be a friend it isn't always easy, but it is a way God can transform us.

If you are struggling in this area of friendships, it may be that you need to prayerfully consider which people you need to invest the most time in. Do your friends speak encouraging truth to you or do you have friends who 'drag you down' with their constant negativity? Are those you spend most time with actually feeding your mask-wearing tendencies, as those I listened to early on in my marriage did? None of the unhelpful ways described in these few paragraphs are how Jesus treats us, so let's take a closer look at how he conducted his friendships.

Friendship 'Jesus style'

God created humans because he wanted a relationship with us, and the first thing we can see when looking at Jesus' life is that he operated in community. He had friends! Did they always lovingly support him? No. As I indicated in Chapter 3, they let him down right in his hour of need – when he was wrestling in the Garden of Gethsemane. So often they blew it, but I think that is because they didn't fully understand his mission; it was so different from what they had been taught to expect. But Jesus still chose to 'do life' with others. He didn't give up on that when people didn't understand him – or when they hurt him. He was obviously also someone people wanted to be around, as he had a large group of followers.

It is interesting to note that he drew a closer group of twelve around him – and he did so after spending the night in prayer (see Luke 6:12–16). That's a great starting point for choosing friends. As human beings we all have a particular capacity for deeper friendships. While we may influence many more people in our day-to-day lives through our interactions at work, home, church and in the wider community, we can't have that deep emotional commitment to more than a small core group. Jesus may have spent hours teaching the crowds around him, but we see that he explained things more deeply to his twelve disciples and allowed them to ask specific questions (see Matt. 13/Mark 4).

In fact, we can see in Jesus' life that, while he did indeed choose those twelve, he actually prioritized the friendship of three of the men within that twelve.[1] He spent most time with Peter, James and John and this seemed totally natural – there are no apologies or explanations for it in Scripture. For example, he took them in to see Jarius's daughter being healed (see Mark 5:37) and up the mountain to witness the transfiguration (see Matt. 17:1) while leaving the rest behind. Jesus was close to a few people, but his approach was loving, relational, open and honest to all those around him.

I think the model of twelve disciples with an inner circle of three reinforces for us that we can't have a level of true intimacy and vulnerability with everyone in our church. If even Jesus focused on three friendships, then I think this is a good model for us to try to reflect in our own lives. By prioritizing a few friendships from within our wider circle, we can begin to really input into one another's lives well; being supportive and encouraging as well as challenging when necessary. This does mean being willing to involve our friends in our everyday lives and activities, which I know can be a challenge in our Western lifestyles today.

You may be thinking, 'That's easier said than done. I just don't feel like there's anyone I click with in my church. As for picking a few friends to go deeper with, I'd love to have even one person who noticed if I was there or not.' If that's you, the experience of my friend Jennie may help.

Jennie was a member of a large, friendly church. She had received a great welcome when she joined, and was part of a mid-week Bible study group. Everyone there was at a very different life stage from her, though, and, while they were all very nice, there were definite friendship groups and Jennie didn't fit into any of them. If she tried to arrange to have coffee with someone, it would be three weeks before they could find a mutually convenient time, though the friends managed to see each other multiple times a week. It all came to a head one Sunday when Jennie walked into church and looked around for a seat. Jennie says:

As usual, the people from my study group were all sitting in clusters with their other friends, and I couldn't see any space near them. I found a seat on my own and slumped into it, feeling very lonely and sorry for myself. During worship, God spoke to me very clearly: 'If you're feeling lonely, don't you think there might be others who are feeling the same? How about you stop focusing on yourself and find a way to make church a better experience for them, instead?'

I signed up to join the Welcome Team and, although I still never developed a big group of friends, I did find one or two who I could be a friend to, and who over the years became people I could also confide in.

I still longed and prayed for at least one really deep friendship, and it was several lonely years before that prayer was answered. One day, however, it landed in my lap out of the blue, in the form of an email from a total stranger who I very quickly 'just clicked' with. She is someone I can be completely honest with, and I'm very thankful to God for her.

As Jennie experienced, sometimes God asks us to step out of our comfort zones, to be the solution for a problem we initially felt only we had. I also love the other lesson I can draw from what she has shared: that sometimes God provides friends in unexpected ways!

Stepping out

As I've said, there is always an element of risk within relationships, but taking that step of vulnerability gives us an opportunity for a level of mutual support that we wouldn't otherwise have. It is good to be intentional about our friendships though. Proverbs 13:20 says: 'Walk with the wise and become wise, for a companion of fools suffers harm.' If you aren't sure which of your friends you could be totally honest with, can I suggest that you take some time to prayerfully reflect on which ones bless you when you spend time with them, so you feel refreshed afterwards, and which drain you. There needs to be a balance – of you being a good friend and supporting others, but also receiving the support that you need.

My prayer is that you will have those you know you can be open with and, if that is the case, perhaps you could spend time with them talking through some of the issues that God has highlighted for you while reading this book. You could ask them to pray and stand with you as you seek to remove your masks and live more authentically.

If you do not have anyone you feel comfortable being that open with, I pray that you will be able to find someone. I know that we cannot force friendship, but asking God first and foremost for his guidance is the best way forward – and I do believe that he will answer. I can remember walking into the church that was to become our spiritual home as a family when we first moved back from America. Aged 11, I was totally bowled over when twins my age rushed over to me and said, 'We've been praying for a friend – and now you've come!' A somewhat overwhelming welcome, but they had had no one else their age in that church for a long time, and so had been praying week after week for God to bring a friend to them. They did in fact become firm friends of mine and, as our youth group began to grow, one of them in particular remained one of my closest friends throughout that period of my life.

When you begin to forge a deeper friendship with someone, it is always helpful to talk about your expectations for the relationship up front. This can ensure you are on the same page. Then give yourselves time to discover if this will be a trusting relationship that you are both totally invested in. I'd also add: be gracious towards one another!

It is such a joy to walk through life with people that we know will encourage and spur us on – those who will also have the grace and sensitivity to simply sit in silence and hug us when we are really hurting and need to express that pain. God created us to be in community. That is why I really do believe that this whole journey of discovering why we wear masks and learning to take them off is so much more manageable when we have a trusted friend by our side that we can share with. Someone who won't judge us, but will stand with us however long it takes.

We may have to take our mask off bit by bit and, just like peeling off a face mask, at times it may be quite painful, so we need someone we can lean on. It may be that

> Friendship is one of God's tangible means of doing us good throughout our lives.

our mask is something we still find convenient and pick it up far too easily. We need that trusted friend to speak the truth to us in love, as God calls us to (see Eph. 4, particularly verse 15). Friendship is one of God's tangible means of doing us good throughout our lives. As we learn how to be good friends to others, and receive their love and support in return, we experience the joy of community.

Personal reflection

'Your friend is the man who knows all about you and still loves you.'

Elbert Hubbard, *The Note Book*, 1927

'Two are better than one, because they have a good return for their labour: if either of them falls down, one can help the other up.'

Ecclesiastes 4:9–10

'One who has unreliable friends soon comes to ruin, but there is a friend who sticks closer than a brother.'

Proverbs 18:24

'Greater love has no one than this: to lay down one's life for one's friends.'

John 15:13

'The blessing it is to have a friend to whom one can speak fearlessly on any subject; with whom one's deepest as well as one's most foolish thoughts come out simply and safely.

Oh, the comfort – the inexpressible comfort of feeling safe with a person.'

                    Dinah Craik, *A Life for a Life*[2]

Read through the above quotes on friendship, and then take some time to write down what you think makes a good friend.

Consider these questions:

• Do you believe you are a good friend to those around you?
• How can you further cultivate trust and safety in your friendship circle?
• If you don't feel you have the close friendships you long for, what could you do to show others that you are a safe person to confide in?

Pray that God will help you to become, or continue to be, the best friend you can be. Ask for his wisdom if you are aware you may have been spending more time with those who pull you down rather than encourage you. Ask him to help you invest more time in those who will champion you and who you, in turn, can support.

Free to Be

In discovering who I am beneath the mask I used to wear, I am finding that God has some very different ideas about who I am called to be. They are so exciting, energizing (and yes, sometimes a tad scary – in a good way!). This doesn't mean that when we remove our masks he expects us to be someone other than who we think we are. Everyone's experience will be different; I'm simply sharing what has happened to me. I *do* think that there can be things lying dormant within us that we just don't realize are there – or have allowed fear to squash down. I know that there have been so many opportunities over the years that I have disqualified myself from grasping hold of, even though I really wanted to pursue them. And others that I kept running away from.

When I was first asked to join a worship team in church, I used to sit up all of Saturday night crying because I was petrified at the thought of playing in front of people. The poor band leader would get a call from me most Sunday mornings saying I couldn't possibly play after having no sleep. Well, God had other ideas. He didn't give up on me (and neither did that wonderful band leader) and took me on a gentle journey, building my confidence.

Today I have the privilege of serving our local church regularly through worship leading, playing keyboard and singing. I also have overall responsibility for our worship team. If someone had told me years ago that I would be doing all this, I probably would have laughed in their face. Yet even in more recent moments of self-doubt, there have been consistent words from various different people that have confirmed that God has indeed called and gifted me to serve in this area. It is certainly something I feel passionate about, and serving others in this way energizes me, even though it takes up a lot of time and effort.

I can see, as I look back over my life, how I liked to be in the background – but God has gently brought me forward in a few particular areas (while graciously allowing me to stay in the background in others). My career choice, for instance, was that of editor (something I still do – and enjoy). However, it was opportunities God brought about, rather than ones I sought, which started me writing. For so long I had worked behind the scenes, helping authors to shape their work so that it could be the best it could be. Then God began pushing me to take that more vulnerable step of being the one creating the words on the page in the first place!

The same has been the case with speaking. When my husband first started encouraging me to speak at church, I resisted but, bit by bit, the opportunities started appearing to speak in other contexts too. Of course, to begin with, part of me responded by telling myself – and God – that I couldn't possibly do it. That there are far too many wonderful extroverts out there who are so natural, so funny – why would people want to hear me? I could certainly relate to how Moses responded to God's calling: 'Pardon your servant, Lord. I have never been eloquent... Please send someone else' (Exod. 4:10,13). But God has been speaking to me about how I have unique things to bring to what he is inviting me to do and, rather than compare myself to others, I should rest in that knowledge. He knows us better than we know ourselves, and he knows that comparison is still something that I can struggle with. But when we learn to fix our eyes on him, rather than those around us, we can gain the confidence to step into all that he has for us.

Embracing ourselves

I now truly believe that I *do* have something unique to offer – with my personality make-up and traits. The adventure of embracing all that he has called me to be is really liberating. The sense of purpose and wellbeing is immense and I have experi-

> The adventure of embracing all that he has called me to be is really liberating.

enced an inner peace and rest even in the midst of busy times when I have been doing what he has asked me to.

The truth is, each one of us is 'fearfully and wonderfully made' (Ps. 139:14). We are unique and reflect the creativity of our God. Just think about fingerprints – no two are the same. In fact, forensics show that even the fingerprints of identical twins are different.[1] How incredible! God fashioned us with such amazing, intricate detail and loves to show his care and love to us (see Ps. 139; Matt. 6:26–34). We *can* trust him enough to go on an adventure of discovery about what our lives can be like without those masks that hide us away.

Knowing and being known by God – and his children – is such a freeing and exciting way to live. I don't get everything right all the time; and it doesn't mean I am never hurt by anyone. When

I have those moments where it feels like my sense of self is being attacked, or I am tempted to reach for my mask, I know that I can go to a safe place with God and work through how that is making me feel. I do so until I am ready to let it go, receiving God's love afresh. Often I turn to the Psalms,

> Knowing and being known by God – and his children – is such a freeing and exciting way to live.

where the raw emotion seems to mirror my own and where I can take on the encouragement to lift my eyes to heaven and gain God's perspective (as we looked at in Chapter 11).

When I am open with my loved ones and close friends about my struggles, they support me through any pain I am experiencing, but also remind me of who I am in Christ and how precious I am to them – and him. Lowering our masks may make us more vulnerable, but it also makes us able to experience a deeper joy and security in God as we partner with him, and those he has placed around us, in a much more open and honest way.

By God's grace

I love 1 Corinthians 15:9–10, because it shows Paul being confident in the person God has made him to be. In fact, when he was being criticized his response was, 'I care very little if I am judged by you' (1 Cor. 4:3). He was not fearful of what others thought. He also went on to say, 'I do not even judge myself.' He refused to listen to his inner critical voice. I don't think he said this because he was being proud, but because his security was based in Christ rather than himself. He humbly acknowledged where he had come from too, 'I am the least of the apostles and do not even deserve to be called an apostle, because I persecuted the church of God' (1 Cor. 15:9). And yet he could say, with confidence, 'by the grace of God I am what I am' (v.10). It didn't stop him from working hard ('I worked harder than all of them'), but he knew that his identity – and his future – was all down to the grace of God. This absolute confidence in who God says we are is key to staying mask-free.

Remembering well

There will be times where we are tempted to pick up our masks and fall back into old patterns of behaviour. In such moments, what I have found helpful is making space to reflect on how far God has brought me. I certainly wouldn't want to be the same person I was early on in my marriage: full of fear, desperately lonely and looking for acceptance in all the wrong places. Recognizing where we were and how far he has taken us already helps us to remember God's goodness towards us, and reminds us of his commitment to seeing us blossom and become more like Jesus.

What happens if we don't take time to remember? Well, just think about the Israelites. God had listened to their cries for help and delivered them from the Egyptians in the most miraculous way, through plagues and even parting the Red Sea. Their response to seeing their oppressors be overtaken by the waves was to sing a spontaneous song of thanks. And yet, not long afterwards, they started dwelling on the fact that they were now in the desert and didn't have an endless supply of food. The result? They began grumbling, even saying: 'If only we had died by the LORD's hand in Egypt!' (Exod. 16:3). I think sometimes we, too, can look at the difficult circumstances we are in and allow them to colour our view of God and ourselves. We become defeatist rather than trusting him for our future.

I find it interesting that, after Nehemiah had led the remnant back to Jerusalem and rebuilt the temple, the priest Ezra read the Book of the Law at the request of the people. They *wanted* to be reminded of God's faithfulness to them over the generations (Neh. 8). And when they collectively confessed before God, they included a summary of their nation's history with him (Neh. 9). It was important to them to learn from their past.

Reading about their story helps each of us to have a wider perspective too, as we remember God's faithfulness to his people throughout history. Romans 15:4 encourages us to do this, as it says, 'everything that was written in the past was written to teach us, so that through the endurance taught in the Scriptures and the encouragement they provide we might have hope'. One of the purposes of the Bible is to feed us with knowledge of God, providing us with an assurance of his overall perfect plan. I still get overwhelmed when I think about the big story of the Bible – God's plan of salvation and redemption – and how he has invited me to be a part of that story.

Reading the Bible also helps me to keep in mind that I was created for a bigger purpose, which particularly encourages me on days when I am struggling with a difficult circumstance or emotion. Here are a few Scriptures that I love meditating on: 'He chose us in him before the creation of the world' (Eph. 1:4) – before the creation of the world God knew he was going to create me! You and I have been known – planned – for centuries. 'For it is by grace you have been saved, through faith – and this is not from yourselves, it is the gift of God – not by works, so that no one can boast. For we are God's handiwork, created in Christ Jesus to do good works, which God prepared in advance for us to do' (Eph. 2:8–10). You have been fashioned by God and saved by him because he has something special for you, which only you can do.

Reminding ourselves of our own particular history with God helps us to keep trusting and stepping out into the freedom he has for us. Keeping a note of how he has spoken to you as an individual, whether through Scripture, words from others, prophecies and so on, as well as how he has answered prayer, builds faith and trust. I find I can look back through my journal and see examples of God's faithfulness leap out from page after page.

You see, while God doesn't promise us an end to all troubles, he is *totally* trustworthy. In Matthew, Jesus promises: 'Surely I am with you always, to the very end of the age' (Matt. 28:20). Knowing that he is walking with us through every stage and moment of life is such a comfort and encouragement. That Jesus, maker of the heavens and earth, would have come down to earth and allowed himself to take on the sins of all humanity, be crushed and killed so that you and I may be free to find our true selves in him, is mind-blowing. Yesterday, today and tomorrow he looks on each of us lovingly, cherishes us and cheers us on. What a great motivation to lower our masks and be who he created us to be. Here are two other promises Jesus shares with his disciples – and us:

I will not leave you as orphans; I will come to you. Before long, the world will not see me any more, but you will see me. Because I live, you also will live (John 14:18–19).

No longer an orphan, you are a precious, beloved child of God. Adopted into his family, you have a Father you can totally depend upon.

I have come that they may have life, and have it to the full (John 10:10).

Because Jesus lives, you can live freely. You can fully be yourself, submitting to his restoring and transforming power each day. I totally believe that 'he who began a good work in you will carry it on to completion until the day of Christ Jesus' (Phil.1:6).

Personal reflection

I have written a 'statement of confidence' below. Please utilize it if you wish to – or write one that reflects your own personal journey. You may find declaring the statement aloud really helpful (and powerful) as you take those first steps of choosing to walk mask-free:

I am what I am . . . by the grace of God. I choose to believe and accept that God loves me exactly as I am. He also loves me so much that he is committed to transforming me into his Son's likeness. I choose to bask in his love today and look to his opinion only.

I recognize that bringing good friends into my life is one of the ways that God transforms me, and uses me to help transform them too. I will learn to be more open with those I truly trust and will accept their advice and constructive, loving challenge humbly before God – as well as doing the same for them.

Each day I will ask God what it is that he would have me do. I will focus on that rather than allowing others to place demands on me.

I will ask God to search my heart regularly. If he brings to mind those I need to forgive and release, including myself, I will take the time to do so, repenting where necessary. I will not skip over such vital processes any longer, but will seek to walk in tandem with the one who knows me better than I know myself. I am so grateful for the healing work that he has already begun in me – I know he will carry it on until it is complete.

Epilogue

I hope that this book has encouraged you to find out who you truly are behind the mask, and that, if you haven't already got them, you will be able to seek out those wise, godly friends who will support you as you aim to live more authentically. If you would like to, please visit my website www.clairemusters.com, where I hope you will find ongoing encouragement and community. I would also love to hear your stories of restoration and healing as you seek to journey deeper with God.

Acknowledgements

The creating of this book is the culmination of a long journey, which began in my own life, and so there are many people to thank – including you the reader for reading *Taking Off the Mask* right through to the end!

Firstly, thanks to fellow author/editor Amy Boucher Pye, who has always been so supportive of my writing and editorial work. She 'just happened' to mention the subject of my book to Authentic, which is how *Taking Off the Mask* came to find such an appropriate home with them.

The whole Authentic team have been fantastic – thanks especially to Rachael Franklin and Donna Harris for believing in my book as well as Becky Fawcett, Charlotte Cuthbert and Lawrie Stenhouse.

My wonderful editor, Jennie Pollock – you edited with such sensitivity and still managed to tighten the writing up. Thank you for your professional touch. Retelling a Bible story is never going to be the same again!

My beta readers, Jennie again, plus Becca and Joanna. Thank you for your honest feedback; it was invaluable.

To Jeff Lucas: thank you for so graciously letting me share about my own book idea when I was editing one of yours. You offered to look at some sample chapters and then commented that you would be pleased to write the foreword, but only if I wanted you to. That was such a fantastic blessing for me!

I also have to mention Ali Hull, who gave me extremely direct feedback early on in my journey of writing this book. It was hard at the time, but I am so very grateful Ali.

To all those who agreed to contribute to the book, either with comments or a personal story – thank you; you have added an extra dimension. I am so grateful for the wisdom shared, and appreciate the courage it took some of you to write what you did.

To my family: Mum, Dad and Vicki, you have always been so supportive of what I do, and you have taught me what it means to be strong and reliable in the face of immense difficulties.

To Emily and Ben – when you are a little older I will give you a copy of this book to read. I hope it may help you avoid some of the mistakes I have made, but most of all will show you how much you are loved by your heavenly Father. It is in him that true freedom is found and I pray that you will keep your eyes firmly fixed on him. I am so grateful to God for the restoration work he did in my life and Dad's – without it we wouldn't have been blessed with two such wonderful children. You do shine a mirror into my soul at times, but you make me smile every single day – I love you.

Steve, I know that we would not be where we are today without your unfaltering love and the grace that you have shown me. As I say in the book, you revealed Jesus' love to me in a way I'd never experienced before. Thank you for your continued grace – even though you are a very private person you have allowed me to share our story as I have felt God prompt me to. Thank you for your support each and every day.

To my River Church Sutton family: I am so honoured that I get to share life with you week by week, learning more together about what it means to follow Jesus and walk further into the freedom he won for us. Thank you for your support.

To those friends who showed us such grace and mercy through our difficulties – thank you for your consistency. I must mention Pete and Mary, as we are so grateful for your loving pastoring.

Finally, God, I know I am nothing without you and I am so grateful for the way you anchor my life. May you take this small offering and use it for your glory . . .

Notes

1 Donning My Mask

[1] This was accompanied by the verse Joel 2:25. In this Old Testament passage, the prophet Joel linked the several years of locusts destroying crops with God's judgement. God promised to restore his people and provide an abundant crop, as they repented.

2 My Unmasking

[1] The rest of the team very graciously worked things round my husband's crazy working hours. Leaders' meetings usually happened on a Saturday brunchtime, to give him a chance to catch up on some sleep first!

4 Discovering Reasons for Our Masks

[1] The survey involved just over 270 people from various churches and denominations around Great Britain.

5 The Role of Upbringing

[1] Chris Ledger and Claire Musters, *Insight into Managing Conflict*, p.35, copyright © 2014 CWR. Used with permission.

[2] For further details see Paul R. Peluso, Jennifer P. Peluso, Janine P. Buckner, Roy M. Kern, William Curlette, 'Measuring Lifestyle and Attachment: An Empirical Investigation Linking Individual Psychology and Attachment Theory', *Journal of Counseling and Development : JCD*, Vol. 87, No. 4 (Fall 2009).

[3] An article based on Sue Gerhardt's verbal presentation to the Quality of Childhood Group in the European Parliament can be found at http://www.ecswe.net/wp-content/uploads/2011/01/QOC2-Chapter3-Why-Love-Matters-How-Affection-Shapes-a-Babys-Brain-by-Sue-Gerhardt.pdf.

[4] Psychologists Brendan Callaghan and René Spitz are quoted by Sara Savage and Eolene Boyd-MacMillan in *The Human Face of Church* (Norwich: Canterbury Press, 2011).

[5] Although, as I mention elsewhere, having two dads did confuse me, particularly in my teenage years.

[6] Joy Lenton blogs at http://www.wordsofjoy.me/ and is also the author of the self-published volume *Seeking Solace* (2016).

[7] We have co-written three books together.

[8] Chris Ledger and I explore the concept of our inner critical voice in more depth in our book *Insight into Self-acceptance* (Farnham: CWR, 2016).

6 Personality Types

[1] Susan Cain provides a great description of extroverts and introverts in *Quiet* (London: Penguin, 2012), pp. 123–124.

² Susan charts this extensively through looking closely at the history of the Culture of Personality within America, showing how gregariousness has come to be viewed as desirable.

³ Think of Bill Gates or J.K. Rowling – both hugely successful thinkers and shapers of culture . . . and both introverts.

⁴ See Sara Savage and Eolene Boyd-MacMillan, *The Human Face of Church* (Norwich: Canterbury Press, 2011), p. 10, where they cite the ideas of D. Rowe, *Beyond Fear* (London: Fontana 1987).

⁵ Will Van der Hart, 'How to befriend the creative mind', Worship Central Conference, Holy Trinity Brompton, 2014. Available at https://www.worshipcentral.org/life/article/befriending-creative-mind-wcconf-14.

⁶ Chris Ledger and Claire Musters, *Insight into Managing Conflict*, p. 55, copyright © 2014 CWR. Used by permission.

7 Influenced by Our Culture

¹ Just watch the adverts in between a TV show intentionally and make a note of the messages they are sending. I get particularly riled by the ads on children's TV, which are certainly geared at getting children to nag their parents for more toys! Although our son is now of an age where computers are of more interest than toys, I am still concerned about the influence our culture is having on him. While he is generally very generous, he doesn't seem to understand the value of money – or of waiting. In my childhood, we saved for whatever it was we wanted – or waited for a birthday or Christmas to ask for it. These days, there seems to be a sense of entitlement that is rubbing off onto our children. With the rise of credit cards and a 'must have now' mindset, kids seem to expect to be able to have whatever they want whenever they want it. Standing up against this is made more difficult when everyone

around them is allowed the very things they want. It just reveals to me the shift in culture within our society.

2   While editing *Am I Beautiful?* I was fascinated to read that when the author, Chine, travelled to Israel she forgot her foundation. I could really connect with that feeling of terror when she realized, and discovered she would not be able to get any suitable replacement. But then she felt challenged to remind herself she *is* beautiful, and to simply go out as she was. When she turned up to meet the rest of the group, no one noticed she was foundation-free! This gave her the idea, once back home, to have a day in which she went to work make-up free too. You can read more about this in Chapter 3 of Chine Mbubaegbu's *Am I Beautiful?* (Milton Keynes: Authentic, 2013). I can also remember the #nomakeupselfie trend, during which I looked at the pictures of women I know without make-up on with interest. They all looked beautiful. So I decided to take the plunge too. I didn't like any of my first few attempts and ended up taking one in such shadow that you could hardly make out my face at all!

3   See http://www.independent.co.uk/life-style/fashion/features/mens-grooming-is-now-a-multi-billion-pound-worldwide-industry-a6813196.html (accessed 13 March 2017).

4   For more details, see Hanna Krasnova, Helena Wenninger, Thomas Widjaja and Peter Buxmann, 'Envy on Facebook: A Hidden Threat to Users' Life Satisfaction?' https://www.researchgate.net/publication/256712913_Envy_on_Facebook_a_hidden_threat_to_users%27_life_satisfaction, (accessed 15 July 2016).

5   Chine is now married, so, while her book still says Mbubaegbu, the endorsement from her at the start of the book is under her new name of McDonald.

6   Esther Emery, *What Falls From the Sky* (Grand Rapids, MI: Zondervan, 2016).

8 Fear of What Others Think

[1] I first read about this in Esther Fleece's book *No More Faking Fine* (Grand Rapids, MI: Zondervan, 2017).

9 Fear of Rejection

[1] Russell Willingham, *Relational Masks* (Downers Grove, IL: InterVarsity Press, 2004), p. 40.

[2] A report on the Proceedings of the National Academy of Sciences of the United States of America website summarizes what they have found and exactly how they researched this:

We demonstrate that when rejection is powerfully elicited . . . areas that support the sensory components of physical pain (secondary somatosensory cortex, dorsal posterior insula) become active. We demonstrate the overlap between social rejection and physical pain in these areas by comparing both conditions in the same individuals using functional MRI. We further demonstrate the specificity of the secondary somatosensory cortex and dorsal posterior insula activity to physical pain by comparing activated locations in our study with a database of over 500 published studies. Activation in these regions was highly diagnostic of physical pain, with positive predictive values up to 88%. These results give new meaning to the idea that rejection 'hurts'. They demonstrate that rejection and physical pain are similar not only in that they are both distressing – they share a common somatosensory representation as well.

Taken from Ethan Kross, Marc G. Berman, Walter Mischel, Edward E. Smith and Tor D. Wager, 'Social rejection shares somatosensory representations with physical pain' – see http://www.pnas.org/content/108/15/6270.full?sid=758b.

3	Margery Williams, *The Velveteen Rabbit* (Heinemann, 1922). Available online at http://digital.library.upenn.edu/women/williams/rabbit/rabbit.html (accessed 15 June 2017).

4	Philip Yancey, *What's So Amazing About Grace?* (Grand Rapids, MI: Zondervan, 1997).

5	Quote by David Taylor found online at http://208.106.253.109/essays/the-little-things-a-meditation-on-the-art-of-encouragement.aspx?page=5.

10 Shame and Guilt

1	What is so wonderful is that, as Amy Boucher Pye reminds us in her book *The Living Cross*, David isn't labelled an adulterer and murderer in the Bible. He truly experienced God's forgiveness and walked in close step with him. Amy Boucher Pye, *The Living Cross* (Abingdon: BRF, 2016), p.74.

2	Carrie Lloyd, *The Virgin Monologues* (Milton Keynes: Authentic Media, 2014).

3	Will van der Hart and Rob Waller, *The Guilt Book* (Nottingham: IVP, 2014), p. 42.

4	Sometimes the things we are feeling guilty or shameful about are life-changing issues that we need expert help with. Here are some great initiatives/organizations for which I have received personal recommendations:

	Porn is increasingly an issue for women as well as men and Naked Truth run online support groups: http://thenakedtruthproject.com.

	Care has an initiative called 'Open' supporting women in the church who have had an experience of abortion but feel church is the very last place they can talk about it: http://weareopen.org.uk.

	Mercy UK has a help line that can refer people (male and female) to other organizations. They also provide prayer, encouragement, advice and resources, as well as a residential Christian disciple programme for women aged 18–30 struggling with eating disorders, self-harm, abuse, etc: http://www.mercyuk.org.

Lifecentre in Chichester, UK helps those who have been sexually abused: http://lifecentre.uk.com. They also have a national helpline.

An online course for those working through trauma, based on Dan Allender's *The Wounded Heart* can be found at: https://theallendercenter.org/offerings/online-courses/healing-the-wounded-heart/.

5 I first came across a similar suggestion in a reflection by Jennifer Rees Larcombe in BRF's Bible study notes *Day by Day with God* (Abingdon: BRF, Sept–Dec 2016).

11 Disappointment

1 Interestingly, her name may mean 'flight' in Hebrew – something she lived up to!
2 This is discussed in reference to church by van der Hart and Waller in *The Guilt Book*, p. 87.
3 Once someone who is hurting has opened up to us, if we aren't sure what to do, we need to ask their permission to seek advice from others.
4 Jennifer runs Beauty from Ashes, a charity that offers prayer ministry to those feeling broken – through individual appointments and retreat days. You can find out more at http://www.beautyfromashes.co.uk or on her Facebook page at https://www.facebook.com/beautyfromashesJRL/.
5 Mark shares a story of his own disappointment in ministry and then asks, 'How might your disappointment invite you to see God, yourself and others more honestly?' What a soul-searching question . . . Mark Yaconelli, *The Gift of Hard Things* (Downers Grove, IL: InterVarsity Press, 2016).
6 Sarah Walton and Kristen Wetherell, *Hope When It Hurts* (Epsom: The Good Book Company, 2017), p. 57.
7 See http://www.bbc.co.uk/news/uk-38516389 for more on her story (accessed 13 February 2017).

8   This is based on teaching I have heard from Wendy Mann, ideas covered in her book *Naturally Supernatural* (Welwyn Garden City: MDP, 2015) and personal discussions with her, as well as other nuggets of wisdom I have picked up from other sources.

9   You can read more about this in Chapter 4 of Esther Fleece, *No More Faking Fine* (Grand Rapids, MI: Zondervan, 2017).

12 Church Culture

1   Stephen Mattson, 'Christianity is Harder Than We Pretend it is', *Relevant*, Issue 70, July/Aug 2014: http://www.relevantmagazine.com/god/christianity-harder-we-pretend-it

2   I find Stephen's comments incredibly helpful:

Contrary to a life of ease, comfort and luxury, following Jesus demands sacrifice, honesty, vulnerability, conflict and a lifetime dedicated to loving others. This is really hard – a commitment not meant to be taken lightly . . .

Unfortunately, many believers are afraid to admit this. We Christians have become experts at putting up a facade of happiness and bliss, pretending that nothing bad ever happens.

We assume that if people find out things aren't all right – that our lives are actually chaotic, messy and out of control, that our relationships are broken, our feelings hurt and that we're filled with worry and pain – they'll get scared away. So we hide these things with the mistaken belief that we're glorifying God – protecting Him from bad press.

But in doing so, we dishonor God and set ourselves up for failure.

3   Sarah Walton and Kristen Wetherell, *Hope When It Hurts*, p. 232.

4   See Phil Moore, *Straight to the Heart of Revelation* (Oxford: Monarch Books, 2010), pp. 87–88.

5   Jacob walked away with a dislocated hip and permanent limp!

13 The Mask Becomes Our Identity

[1] I read about this in Linda Douty, *How Can I Let Go If I Don't Know I'm Holding On? Setting Our Souls Free* (New York, NY: Morehouse Publishing, 2005). She goes on to explain how loss and gain pervade every area of our lives. For example, in developmental areas: we learn to let go of clinging to our mother to become more independent in infancy; as older adolescents we often move away from home to make our own way in the world. Psychologically, we learn to let go of some of the things that are beyond our control but which would tie us up in knots if we keep hold of them – such as a need to always be right, for the world to always be fair. In the spiritual life there is a letting go in order to gain (see Mark 8:35). Water baptism also can be a symbol of us 'dying' to our old self, and being raised in Christ. This all fits with the idea of us letting go of barriers between us and God so we can receive more of the fullness of his love and grace.

[2] Linda's book *How Can I Let Go If I Don't Know I'm Holding On?* includes an explanation of the difference between roles and masks, which I found helpful.

PART THREE: REMOVING THE MASK

[1] Lucy Mills, *Forgetful Heart* (London: Darton, Longman and Todd, 2014), pp. 18–19.

14 Remember Who You Are

[1] http://www.adweek.com/adfreak/dove-hires-criminal-sketch-artist-draw-women-they-see-themselves-and-others-see-them-148613 (accessed 15 June 2015).

2 Arianna Walker, *Mirror Image: Breaking Free from False Reflections* (Oxenhope: Presence Books, 2011).
3 The list I am referring to can be found at https://www.ficm.org/handy-links/#!/who-i-am-in-christ
4 A really helpful book that explores this subject is R.T. Kendall, *Your Words Have Power* (London: Hodder & Stoughton, 2006).

15 It Takes Courage to Remove the Mask

1 Joanna Weaver, *Having a Mary Heart in a Martha World* (Colorado Springs, CO: WaterBrook Press, 2000).

16 The Support of Friends

1 It was my good friend Akhtar Shar who first brought this to my attention.
2 Dinah Craik, *A Life for a Life* (Leipzig: Bernhard Tauchnitz, 1859)

17 Free to Be

1 http://www.encyclopedia.com/social-sciences-and-law/law/crime-and-law-enforcement/fingerprint (accessed 20 February 2017).